THE
FFESTINIOG RAILWAY

Volume 2

• A PAST AND PRESENT COMPANION •

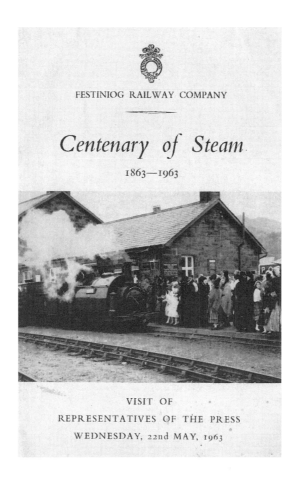

FESTINIOG RAILWAY COMPANY

Centenary of Steam

1863—1963

VISIT OF
REPRESENTATIVES OF THE PRESS
WEDNESDAY, 22nd MAY, 1963

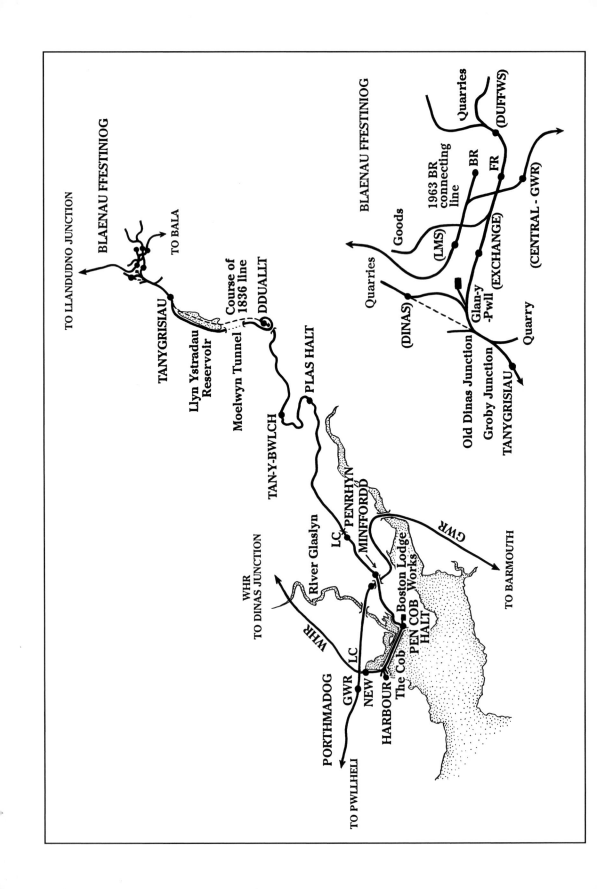

THE
FFESTINIOG
RAILWAY

Volume 2

· A PAST and PRESENT COMPANION ·

A second nostalgic journey along the line from Porthmadog to Blaenau Ffestiniog

John Stretton

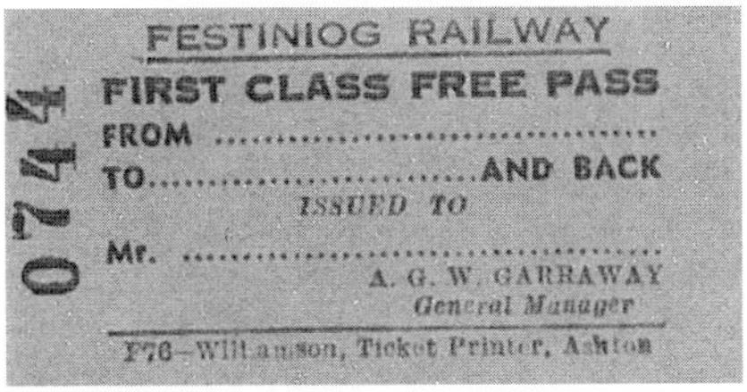

FESTINIOG RAILWAY
FIRST CLASS FREE PASS
FROM ....
TO.....................AND BACK
ISSUED TO
Mr. ....
A. G. W. GARRAWAY
General Manager
F76—Williamson, Ticket Printer, Ashton

0744

· RAILWAY HERITAGE ·
from
The NOSTALGIA Collection

First published in 2005

British Library Cataloguing in Publication Data

A catalogue record for this book is available from the British Library.

ISBN 1 85895 234 4

Past & Present Publishing Ltd
The Trundle
Ringstead Road
Great Addington
Kettering
Northants NN14 4BW

Tel/Fax: 01536 330588
email: sales@nostalgiacollection.com
Website: www.nostalgiacollection.com

Map by Christina Siviter

Printed and bound in Great Britain

Past and Present

A Past & Present book
from
The NOSTALGIA *Collection*

ACKNOWLEDGEMENTS

This has been another challenging but highly enjoyable project and I would like immediately to thank all on the FR who have given me time, co-operation, courtesy and assistance, in whatever form. Without the railway's help a book like this could not be successfully completed. Thanks also go to the many photographers who have entrusted their precious illustrations to my care, sometimes for many years! Those whose photographs are used are duly credited, but they are all hereby thanked – their trust and patience is truly appreciated. A special mention should be made of: Paul Davies, Allan Garraway and Adrian Gray, who have all picked over and proof-read my poor attempts at accurate and informative captions!; Hilary Davies, for her hospitality and superb food; Fred Howes, for his assistance; all at Silver Link for their part in the production; my daughter Tammy, whose love of the FR still burns strong; and my wife, Judi, who again has borne the loss of me to a computer and hundreds of photographs strewn across the floor! Without them all this book would not have seen the light of day.

CONTENTS

A steamy evocation of 'then and now' on the FR. Representing times past, *Merddin Emrys*, a product of the original Festiniog Railway in 1879, takes water at the 'new' water tower at Tan-y-bwlch, a 1990 replacement for the original that stood just out of the picture to the left. Driver Colin Dukes watches as the water fills *Merddin*'s tank – and not the chimney as it would appear! – during a stop at the station while operating the 1045 Porthmadog-Blaenau Ffestiniog service on 27 August 1994. *MJS*

INTRODUCTION

As I write in 2004, the Ffestiniog Railway is recovering from turbulent times – but it was ever thus, as the railway, both before and following restoration, has had challenges, setbacks and times of opposition and/or hard choices. It has always been at the forefront of development and innovation – ever since Stephenson derided the idea of running steam locomotives on a 2-foot gauge over such demanding terrain as lay between Blaenau Ffestiniog and Porthmadog. That innovation and market-leading ideas continue, with, in 2004, the introduction of 'The Talking Train', a product that has no equal in the railway world. This is especially needed as, on the ground, there has been no major change in route layout, and this could lead to a falling away of public interest – however, with a band of enthusiastic, far-seeing, media-and-finance-savvy people now in charge, the future looks happier than in the recent past.

Happily for your author, there has been much progress and development on the railway over the past half-century and the photographs contained in this volume highlight much of that. Tackling any project such as this, for which you have an in-built attraction, is a labour of love. It is also, however, a labour of guilt and sadness, as many excellent illustrations that

A relatively early view of the resurrected railway: on 8 October 1955, during the first Special Meeting of the Ffestiniog Railway Society, members of the Society gather at Portmadoc – then still with its Anglicised spelling – before *Prince* takes them on a trip up the line. Fireman Arwyn Morgan (a Boston Lodge apprentice at the time) watches and waits from *Prince*'s cab, while driver and Manager Allan Garraway discusses some point with FR Company directors Trevor Bailey (left) and Les Smith. Note Trevor's delightful Sunbeam in the car park, which in those days came right up to the rear of the platform. *MJS collection*

Close to three decades on from the picture on the previous page, the railway has regained access to Blaenau Ffestiniog and has transformed itself from an 'enthusiasts' pipe-dream' to a professionally run public service that is the envy of the preservation world. On 30 August 1982 *Mountaineer* leaves Harbour station in Porthmadog in glorious sunshine and heads towards some decidedly threatening clouds, forming the 1550 special departure for the Bristol Railway Circle, with Observation Car No 11 at the rear. *Peter Treloar*

truly deserve to be seen are of necessity squeezed out by the limited availability of space. For around 120 'past' photographic spaces I had in the region of 700 prints – and that is ignoring colour slides that I knew were available! Something had to give and I crave the indulgence of those photographers who have suffered in the cull. Similarly, I have attempted to avoid inclusion of previously published material wherever possible and have also excluded views that would have been very similar to some in Volume 1. Neither have I attempted to give a full textual history of the images herein, as much of this narrative is available from that earlier and other volumes; also, I have referred throughout to Porthmadog, rather than the original 'Portmadoc', as the 'Welshification' of the name took place during the period covered by this book and I felt that trying to label the pictures in their appropriate time frame could be both confusing and potentially inaccurate. Again, I ask forgiveness if this offends.

2004 saw the 50th anniversary of the inheritance of the FR by the enthusiasts, and the celebrations for this – and the similar 'birthday' of the first train in 1955 – will go some way to counter the media attention given to the current exciting and wonderful rebuilding of the Welsh Highland Railway. Both are magnificent, world-beating enterprises and deserve to be enjoyed by the widest possible audience. Those familiar with the FR will know what there is to see and love, but if you are a newcomer to the railway let me, through this book, help to introduce you to it and encourage you to explore it more thoroughly. You will not be disappointed – and should you wish to be personally involved, you can be sure of a very warm welcome!

M. John Stretton

Porthmadog

In the early days of restoration, there was great need to return as much as possible of the previous railway's equipment to working condition. Some items were beyond recall and were cut up, sold for scrap or otherwise disposed of, but wherever possible repair was the order of the day. Much initiative and improvisation was called for and, thankfully, at times this was present in abundance. A makeshift sheer-leg device has been erected on 19 October 1958 to lift ailing coal wagon No 19 on to the waiting H. Pountney Ltd lorry, before making the journey to Birmingham for rebuilding. The day's operations, hauling the wagon along the ex-WHR track seen in the foreground, began in inclement weather – note the water between the rails – but were blessed with much better conditions as work progressed. A café forms the far end of Britannia Terrace, a welcome venue for volunteers – and where several marriages had their beginnings!

The same vantage point on 1 May 2004 displays the many changes and developments that have taken place over the ensuing 45-plus years. The old connecting link to the WHR was removed fairly early on in the restoration period, when it was realised that there was then no foreseeable possibility of re-introducing a service towards Beddgelert; the café has become the renowned Cob Records store; the upper storeys of Britannia Terrace have had dormer windows fitted; and, above all, the level of road traffic has mushroomed, as Porthmadog has become a 'tourist honey-pot'. Still extant, however, are the boundary railings on the right. With plans now to re-instate the rail link, roughly in line with that seen above, it will be interesting to witness the trains threading through the holiday traffic! *Bob Smallman/MJS*

In 1966 the station proudly announces its presence to intending passengers, although the approach is 'rough and ready' in the days before the redevelopment of the slate wharf; note an old wharf building in the centre distance. Boats lie at anchor in the harbour on the right, while the water tower and coaling stage, between the station buildings and the old wharf structure, await the next arrival. The Porthmadog Guides' Hut, which constrained car parking space for years, is just visible on the left.

Both the slate wharf housing development and the need for much more controlled car parking are readily apparent in this May Day picture from 2004. The current locomotive water tank can just be seen to the left of the car park kiosk, and the 'Welshification' of the railway's name has been accomplished with the addition of an 'F' on the station building, but otherwise the vista is dramatically less relaxed than the view above. *Howard Wilson/MJS*

The water tower glimpsed opposite is seen here on the left in closer detail, complete with the signal that indicated how the three-way point was set. In this view, from the late 1950s, Double-Fairlie *Taliesin* has been fed and watered, the fireman has set the points for a return to the station complex, and he prepares to regain his position beside the double firebox. He is watched by a solitary young chap in short trousers, enjoying the lack of barriers keeping him away from either the railway or the harbour behind him! Some of the housing that came with the emergence and importance of shipping in Portmadoc (sic) can be seen in the background, climbing the hill to Borth y Gest.

Within a decade, the railway area had been tidied and the siding to the right of *Taliesin* removed. Before the 21st century – and the requirements of Health & Safety – the railway installed fencing around its boundary at this part of Harbour station, to safeguard and delineate its area of occupation, resulting in a far more clinical feel. Further developments include the provision of a larger water tank and the complete change from the earlier supplies of coal to tank wagons to supply oil-fired locos. Other than the growth of trees and the proliferation of motor cars, exemplified by the one parked on the quayside, the distant view is little changed. *Rev John Parker, Hugh Davies collection/ MJS*

The visit to the water tower/oil tanks is usually the preserve of the locomotive from an incoming service, but on special occasions this can change. On May Day 1988 the sole remaining ex-WHR locomotive *Russell* is a rare visitor to Harbour station and is the subject of much attention. It stands here on the left as *Blanche* and *Mountaineer* move away, having been duly refreshed. *Peter Treloar*

Moving to the water tower and turning through 180 degrees, the unusual triple point is highlighted in the foreground, showing how cramped the site was, limiting locomotive movements. On 31 July 1958 *Prince* stands in the centre of the picture, with *Taliesin* to the right at the coal stage, and the 2.30pm train to Tan-y-bwlch awaiting its motive power; note the Observation Car No 11 on the rear.

With the growth in passenger numbers requiring longer trains, the restricted site at Harbour station needed a rethink. The results can be seen in this view of the site on 1 May 2004, the obvious difference being the loss of the three-way point – moved to a site in Minffordd yard. The yard area has been opened out to give this more flexible arrangement of five sidings. On the right, *Lilla* waits for another visitor to enjoy a 'Drive an Engine' experience, while *Linda* shunts stock and the 1430 service for Blaenau Ffestiniog loads, ready for the off. Note the presence once again of Observation Car No 11, standing under the canopy that now protects waiting passengers. *Henry Priestley, Peter Treloar collection/MJS*

When the original railway ceased operations in 1946, the system was literally abandoned – left like a child's toy that no longer held any fascination! With virtually no attempt at tidying up or storage, locations became 'ghost towns'. This view of Harbour station five years later, on 5 October 1951, shows windows and doors still intact on the main building and stock – predominantly slate wagons – gradually deteriorating, exposed to the elements, while grass is rapidly taking hold of the trackbed. Passenger vehicles had been removed to Boston Lodge by this time.

The position was exactly the same when the restorationists finally gained control in 1954, but by October 1958 – the date of the second view – great strides had been made, not just in restoring locomotives and stock to working condition, but also in progressively clearing the line northwards. Here *Prince* re-enters the station with its short rake, returning from a run to Tan-y-bwlch. Signs of 'progress' are the replacement of the glass in the external light on the station building and the arrival of the first TV aerials on Britannia Terrace in the distance.

Nearly half a century later the transformation is complete. Not only have the original buildings been preserved and adapted to modern usage, but the gap between them has been infilled – by a bookshop and first-floor offices – the trackwork redesigned, and new rolling-stock constructed to complement and integrate with restored and renovated originals – note that No 11 is still hogging the limelight! More TV aerials have sprouted in this view from May 2004 and the dormer window fashion has spread! *Hugh Ballantyne/Mike Esau/MJS*

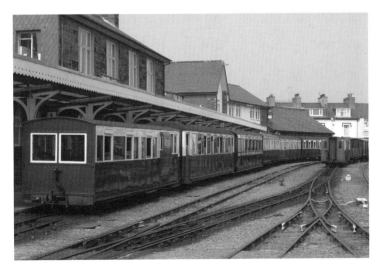

The date of the first photograph is 17 October 1954, and a start has been made on clearing the site. Seen from the opposite end of the station site from the view on the previous page, the curly-roofed brake-van and goods van have been removed to Boston Lodge and work has begun on removing brushwood, etc, from the trackbed. A former slate wagon is in use here as carrier for gas tanks and oxyacetylene cutting equipment. There is obviously much still to do!

Eighteen months later progress is evident. Redundant stock has gone, some by scrapping, being of more value as scrap turned to cash! In a rare view from October 1955, *Prince* – still with his wooden nameplate – has collected a load of wheels from the scrapping operation and added this five-wagon load to the 'end of day' empty stock, ready for the short run across the Cob to Boston Lodge and disposal.

Thirty years later, on 19 April 1986, *Prince* is still hard at work – but now resplendent in a new red coat – with a longer rake of vintage coaching stock, comprising No 16 of 1872, 1863-vintage No 5, and vans 12 and 11, forming the 1140 departure to Minffordd. Note the provision of a raised platform area, evidence of painting on the station building and the provision of yet more dormer windows, this time on the railway itself. The yard is now clear of weeds, but the platform canopy has yet to be erected. *Bob Smallman (2)/Hugh Ballantyne*

Moving further towards Britannia Terrace, this view gives a clearer impression of the original layout of the station, with the goods shed at the near end and the tall starter signal. Though undated, the view is probably around 1949/50, as the grass has really taken hold, but the chest-high fencing between the two buildings – though in a decidedly dilapidated state! – is still in situ; it had disappeared by the time of the 1951 photograph on page 13. Also still in place is the LMS-sponsored notice board, visible just above the fence.

The ensuing 20 years saw much travail and genuine progress and development. *Blanche*, here still a coal-burner, is intent on advertising herself – but probably in flagrant disregard for the Clean Air Act! – as she waits for the 'right away' in 1968, ready to haul her load to Tan-y-bwlch. The tall starter – the post of which had still been in situ a decade earlier – has gone, as have two of the chimney pots on the main building, but the goods shed has had its guttering and downpipes attended to, and poster boards added. The first four coaches are in the mock-teak livery of the period, whereas the final three bear remnants of the previous green and ivory coat. The yard still has the original four roads.

Into the 21st century the old goods shed is now a popular and renowned bar and restaurant, hence the chairs just visible on the right; its poster boards have been breeding, as have the yard tracks; and the new platform is well shown, as is the canopy and the connecting of the two original buildings. Waiting passengers and supporters of the railway enjoy a moment of quiet between services on 1 May 2004. Note the appearance of newer housing on the far side of the harbour. *J. H. Ahern, Peter Treloar collection/Paul Chancellor collection/MJS*

In the first of these two views of Harbour station departures, it is still relatively early days and the volunteers are working hard to cope with the increasing interest and support – victims of their own success! Some time during the summer of 1957, *Prince* takes the strain on the first steps on his journey to Penrhyn. Note the two former signal posts still in place, left and right of *Prince*, and the line to the goods shed and former WHR still surviving, immediately to the right of the train.

By 29 May 1978 change has been dramatic. Not only has steam been temporarily ousted by the railway's Planet diesel *Upnor Castle*, but the trackbed is clean and with a revised layout, there is a fence protecting visitors from the trains, the new 'infill' building is seen on the extreme left, and the number of TV aerials on Britannia Terrace has mushroomed! The 1100 departure enjoys the bright Whitsun Holiday sunshine as it begins its run to Dduallt, then the northern terminus. *Norman Keen/Brian Morrison*

In the early years of the preserved railway, the last yards out of Harbour station saw the trains passing Britannia Foundry, seen here on the right. Serving the town, Blaenau's quarries and the original railway for many decades, the foundry closed in 1965 after its trade had diminished to uneconomical levels, and was demolished in late 1970s. With an ugly Inland Revenue building now in its place, the attractive stone-built works are still much lamented – they might well have become listed if they had survived just a few more years. On 3 September 1972 *Linda* pulls out of the station yard with stock to add to her mid-morning train, which she will guide along the extreme right-hand track and back into the platform to pick up waiting travellers. Note that the English spelling is still present on the nameboard, replaced by the 'Welsh' version in the lower view opposite.

That hideous Revenue building not only stares boldly out to the railway, but has also exposed the very blank end wall of Britannia Terrace! On 9 April 2004 *Prince* does his best to mask this with his exhaust and to enliven the very dull conditions with the 1330 pre-launch run of the 'Talking Train'. This brand new concept from the railway – which has stolen a march on any other line – has given real added value to the railway's experience, offering something truly different to the more usual run up the line. Note the repositioning of the station nameboard on the end wall of Spooner's Bar. *Geoff King/MJS*

Turning through 180 degrees, this is the view from Harbour station across the Cob, the mile-long causeway envisaged by William Madocks and opened, after his death, in September 1811. Separating the sea on the right from the estuary on the left, he created, at a stroke, the opportunity for a railway and a transport corridor for slate from Blaenau Ffestiniog and for the township of Portmadoc. We, the inheritors of his genius and vision, are now able to enjoy visually and physically the many and varied journeys made by the FR. On 8 September 1984 *Mountaineer* approaches its destination on an afternoon service from Blaenau. A solitary pedestrian, beyond the train, shares the joy of the crossing as he walks from Boston Lodge, visible in the distance.

Mountaineer is again the train loco in this view 20 years later, on 1 May 2004, but this time accompanied by the 1992-vintage FR-built Double-Fairlie *David Lloyd George*, as they complete the final few yards to their destination on an afternoon run from the top end of the railway. The rake, however, is 11-strong this time, rather than the mere six coaches seen above! The headboard proudly announces 'See us at Railfest', a reference to the celebration of 200 years of railways to be held at the NRM in York later that month. *Tom Heavyside/MJS*

A few yards further along the Cob, on 29 May 1978, we see the fireman of *Merddin Emrys* in a rather precarious position – presumably attempting some relief from the heat of the fireboxes just inches in front of him! – as his train nears the end of its journey from Dduallt. Note the similarly precarious position of the bathers at the base of the signal post. Perhaps to the relief of the railway, such has been the change in character of the seaward landscape over the intervening years that this scene is hardly likely to be repeated in the 21st century. Out of commission since 2000, *Merddin Emrys*, beloved of so many within and without the FR, is due to be returned to active service during 2005. *Brian Morrison*

In a final look at Porthmadog, from near the middle of the Cob, it is 7 September 1957, towards the end of the season, and *Prince* is about to pass the distinctive three-arm signal that was a feature of this point for so many years. Sadly, the 80-year-old post, which had served at Duffws until 1925, succumbed to a gale early in 1967, although a replacement is still in mind. Notice how quiet the adjoining roadway is on the right!

Fifteen years later, on 3 September 1972, the American Locomotive Company (ALCO) *Mountaineer* has only been on the railway for a couple of years and still has its cab as first adapted. With this angle emphasising the difference in height of the FR's normal stock, it passes the ex-GNR somersault signal, Porthmadog's advanced starter, on its way to Dduallt. Note how the wharf on the left has been transformed with a development of white-coated flats, and that, just discernible on the right, there is now a traffic queue to enter Porthmadog.

There is yet more road traffic on 1 May 2004, although not yet as bad as it was to be later in the day, when the queue to enter the town stretched back to Minffordd, some 3 miles away! Having spent the day giving visitors the chance to drive her, *Lilla* makes a spirited crossing of the Cob at 1547, with just a brake-van in tow, obviously not wishing to be a hindrance to the next up train, the stock for which can be seen waiting in Harbour station in the background. Notice that the white house, predominant to the right in the two earlier views, has gone, demolished with Britannia Foundry. *Brian Pask/ Geoff King/MJS*

Boston Lodge

This superb view of both the Cob – over which the train is passing – and Traeth Mawr, with the eastern edge of Tremadoc centre left beyond, superbly illustrates the scope of the problem facing William Madocks in 1806 and his magnificent achievement, with the whole of the lower half of this picture previously being under tidal water. Seen from high on the spit of land behind Boston Lodge Works, *Merddin Emrys* crosses the Cob with the 1445 service for Blaenau Ffestiniog on 25 October 1990. Note how the silting from the tides against the Cob is gradually reclaiming land from the sea on the near side. *Peter Treloar*

We have now arrived at Boston Lodge Works, so named as William Madocks was MP for Boston in Lincolnshire. With the road following the 90-degree left-hand swing landwards from the Cob and a high wooden fence guarding the Works yard from the running line, *Taliesin* returns from a run to Penrhyndeudraeth – then the terminus – and prepares to take the curve on to the final stretch to Porthmadog on 31 August 1957. Note the quiet road and archway in the retaining wall that once gave access to the Works yard.

A little over a decade later there have been changes. On the significantly widened bend in the road, now marked with white lines, the previous stone wall separating it from the estuary has been replaced by a footpath and fencing. On the railway, the most dramatic development has been the removal of the high fence, giving an open aspect into the yard from passing trains. Negotiating the Boston Lodge curve in 1969, *Mountaineer* is in its first season on the railway, having been acquired by Society Director John Ransom in 1967, and is here coupled to Gardner diesel *Moelwyn* on the return journey from Dduallt. Note the diminutive No 2 van between the locomotives and the coaching stock, deputising for an observation car, and the substantial stone pillar still guarding the entrance to the Works yard.

By 8 June 1995 Boston Lodge cottages, built as barracks for the men building the Cob and now used as staff accommodation by the railway, have had a repaint. The Works' chimney, so long a feature of the Boston Lodge skyline, has gone, as has that on the former Stores in the foreground. The gate pillar has also been removed but a more railway-like fence has been installed beside the main line. *Prince* negotiates the curve with a rake of empty stock on its way to be stored in the Old Engine Shed.
Brian Pask/Jon Marsh/MJS

The first motive power to be resurrected after the restorationists assumed responsibility for the railway in 1954 was a Simplex internal-combustion-engined 'tractor'. Sometime known as *Mary Ann*, it is seen here on the 'main line', on the curve outside the Works yard on 28 June 1956, shunting the newly restored No 11 Brake Third and surrounded by some of the undergrowth that had proliferated during the closure years. The entrance tracks for the yard lie 'embedded' in the earth, with weeds between the rails.

Within two years the trackwork was much improved and movements into the yard and around the curve were more frequent and of greater length. By the time of this view, during a Vintage Weekend in October 1996, track has been both replaced and realigned. *George Sholto*, a visiting engine from the Bressingham Steam Museum in Norfolk, makes its way out of the yard and prepares for the run across the Cob. It is at the head of a rake of mixed freight, hidden behind the generous steam exhaust! *H. C. Casserley, Peter Johnson collection/MJS*

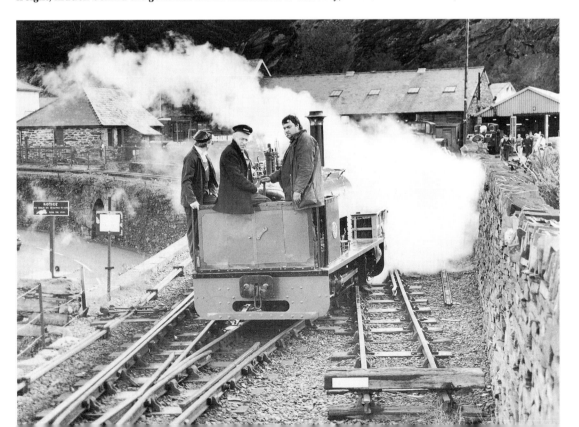

In an undated view from the closure period, a visitor, complete with stick, stands between the Second World War pillbox – a dry-stone structure hardly proof against serious attack! – and the nearer Pen Cob signal box, with just four levers but still a block post in the days before the First War. As we look across the Cob towards Porthmadog and the moody Moel y Gest beyond, there has clearly been rain in the hills, as the Traeth has filled while the tide was in. Note the gap in the wall in the right foreground, giving access to the roadway below. *MJS collection*

By the time of this photograph, which was taken from the top of the stone pillar at the yard entrance in March 1956, the pillbox has been partly demolished, but the signal box and the steps up from the road remain. Great strides have been made in clearing and fettling the running line on the right, whereas the yard tracks still have a covering of sand. *Prince* lazily indulges in a spot of shunting. *Bob Smallman*

The passage of 31 years has seen much improvement, but, like all railways, there is always work to be done! On 26 April 1987 access to the Works yard is temporarily blocked as work begins on demolition of the long-standing pillar, with sleepers laid to protect the pointwork. The two youthful volunteers don't seem to be overworked! Note that Nos 1 and 2 Boston Lodge Cottages, on the left, are now in need of some TLC! *Peter Treloar*

The vantage point above and behind Boston Lodge gives a wonderful vista of both the Works yard and the Cob leading to Porthmadog. Again demonstrating Madocks's wonderful creation – and the encroachment of silt over sand – this view from 29 August 1988 shows the signal box still in place, the steps from the road now partitioned from the running line, and the partially dismantled pillar. It also shows the loco pit, in the centre of the yard, exposed following the demolition of the Long Shed that had previously covered it. *Peter Treloar*

The first of these three views of the Works yard in October 1954 – sadly a slightly damaged print – provides a less common view of the site prior to the arrival of willing hands. What appear to be brambles cover the area between the old tall fencing on the left and the Hearse Van and coaching stock, which could well be in danger from the 'Triffids'! Beyond, the buildings sleep, awaiting their kiss of life.

Trapped between the seaward wall (right) and the wall of the Long Shed (left), slate wagons lie idle on the trackway leading to the Carriage Sheds in Glan-y-mor yard, on the southern edge of the Works complex. It was to be another eight years before real efforts were made to clear this area, though the wagons had been put to use by that time.

Many people, faced with such a view, would have abandoned any idea of restoration, but the 1950s FR volunteers were made of much sterner stuff and the Stores were soon returned to use and the yard in front cleared. Note the wagon turntable, bottom right, and the remains of a lamp standard. *All Bob Smallman*

This wider view of the main yard in 1954 – this time on 24 August – again shows the degree of nature's reclamation after the abandonment in 1946. Various items of rolling-stock populate the yard, with the wall of the Long Shed on the extreme right.

By 1957 the same vantage point looks totally different and much improved. *Taliesin* rests between duties on the 'outside' pit line (left), but other stock is parked around the yard, as a visitor carrying wet-weather gear surveys the scene. Note that the Long Shed has had its door repaired with corrugated iron.

Nearly fifty years later, on 4 May 2004, the view is again changed. Gone are the tall Works chimney and the Long Shed building, leaving the pit on the right clear, while the trackwork has been slightly redesigned. Elsewhere, the former Stores, now an S&T workshop, has had its chimney removed but a porch fitted; the former sawmill between there and the main workshops has been demolished; and these main buildings have been rebuilt following removal of the chimney. In the yard, diesel *Criccieth Castle*, built by the FR in 1995, stands behind K1. The latter, the world's first Garratt locomotive, built in Manchester in 1909, is here in the later stages of full restoration to working order – an event long awaited by many. *H. C. Casserley, Peter Johnson collection/ N. C. Simmons, Hugh Davies collection/ MJS*

Behind the scenes! A view not normally seen by the public, this was the scene in the Top Yard in April 1958, still relatively early days for the new railway. Wagon wheels and the trailing bogie from *Moel Tryfan* stand on tracks in front of the Smithy and iron foundry, while still inactive wagons and box vans line up awaiting attention. The main running line is beyond the buildings to the right. Note the bell post sprouting from the roof in the centre and, to the left, the tall Works chimney. *Palmerston*, on the left, was ensconced in this position for many years as a stationary boiler.

With a road vehicle impeding the 'past' vantage point, this is the view a couple of paces to the right on 4 May 2004. As can be seen, the vast majority of the buildings survive, as do the tracks, although these are no longer in use, but the tall chimney has gone and there has been some development to adapt to modern needs. *Palmerston* has been restored and is again part of the railway's motive power pool. Originally built in 1807, Boston Lodge is now the oldest working railway workshops in the world and, apart from the few brief years from 1946-54, has been in constant daily use. *Rod Blencowe collection, Peter Treloar collection/MJS*

Before the war, on 10 July 1936, Single-Fairlie *Moel Tryfan* stands in the Erecting Shop at Boston Lodge Works, stripped down for attention. Sadly, with the run-down of traffic on the railway, most of which was being handled by *Merddin Emrys*, *Moel Tryfan* was not to work again and, equally sadly, its remains were cut up for scrap in 1954. While regrettable in hindsight, this was necessary at the time, as the restorationists needed both money and space and they had no crystal ball to foresee the wonders that have unfolded over the years.

The low beams seen in the first view are again in evidence here, reinforcing the cramped nature of the Works and the primitive conditions in which employees had to work! On 16 August 1955, Double-Fairlie *Taliesin* is still the proud bearer of its nameplate, in the condition as left in 1946, not having worked since before the Second World War. It was to see the light of day again on 4 September 1956.

During the early 1970s an extension was built at the rear of the workshops, more than doubling the available space; this was essential to cope with the increased demands created by the growing popularity of the railway, the decision to build both a new Double-Fairlie and steel carriages, and the number of its serviceable locomotives. The last 40 years have seen both new build and ongoing repair and restoration of original items, including, in this view from 4 May 2004, the much-loved *Merddin Emrys*. The extra space and improved conditions are self-evident here, with work progressing on *Merddin* towards a 2005 return to traffic. *Maurice Dart collection/Terry Gough/MJS*

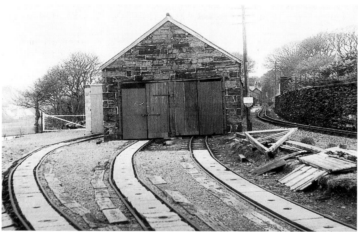

The railway's original engine shed at Boston Lodge, built in 1863, was immediately to the north of the Works, alongside the running line on which the couple are standing in July 1955; the rails are just visible between them and the shed. To their left, long-abandoned coaching stock sits quietly rotting outside the shed entrance.

By 12 April 1975 the view is much changed and the rather untidy appearance of the line at the time is evident. Though not resurrected as an operational engine shed, the new railway has still put the building to good use, as a storage shed for those items not immediately needed or in line for attention and, more recently, for its vintage carriages. The running line is clearly seen on the right, and the blocks between the rails in the yard are to enable road access from the gate on the left, although as yet there is no fencing between the two.

As one more indication of the dedication of the railway's servants, in this view from 8 June 1995 the walls, track and ballast have all received meticulous attention. Passing the old shed wall *David Lloyd George* – new from Boston Lodge in late 1992 – heads for Porthmadog with the 1510 service from Blaenau Ffestiniog. *Maurice Dart collection/ Sydney Leleux/MJS*

The engine shed is seen this time in 'proper' use. Around the turn of the 20th century, three types of locomotive pose with their crews and shed staff. Left to right, they are Single-Fairlie *Taliesin*, Double-Fairlie *Merddin Emrys* and 1863-vintage *Prince*.

On 16 October 1999, as a Vintage Weekend 'special', the above line-up was recreated by the railway, to the delight of staff and volunteers, as well as photographers! *Taliesin* again stands in place – although this time it is the new-build version recently completed at Boston Lodge – with six-year old *David Lloyd George* and a 'genuine article', *Palmerston*, built in 1864 and recently restored. Note the absence of rooftop smoke vents and the shorter left-hand shed compared with the 'past' view. *FR archives/MJS*

Immediately beyond the engine shed was Boston Lodge Halt. Not a hive of activity, it is nevertheless a well-used facility. On 30 August 1955, the date of the first view, it is the temporary terminus while work continues to make the route to Minffordd and beyond suitable for traffic. *Prince* pauses for his admiring public and for photographs.

Due to its clever construction, the whole of the route from Boston Lodge to Blaenau Ffestiniog is on a rising gradient, but this does put some pressure on 'light-footed' locomotives, especially in damp conditions. Such is the case here, on 2 May 1988, during a Gala weekend, as sand is placed on the rails in front of visitor *Russell*, to assist with restarting the 1115 service from Porthmadog.

Even the most powerful FR locomotives have to work hard restarting from Boston Lodge, especially when hauling a fully laden 11-coach train. Happily for the crew of *Earl of Merioneth* on 4 May 2004, the coaches are not that full at 0925 as they restart their journey, and the pull away does not need artificial aids. Note that the site has not changed greatly over the years, with the exception of the provision of a formal platform edge and the growth of tree cover. This latter does not help adhesion! *Eric Bareham/Peter Treloar/MJS*

Another view of *Russell* on 2 May 1988, but this time later in the day. To prevent further problems, *Prince* has been added inside as train engine for the 1650 departure from Porthmadog and the duo gather speed away from the Halt, passing an unusually quiet road. When this stretch of the road is backed up with vehicles waiting to enter Porthmadog, their occupants can enjoy the tantalising vision of the trains at this clear spot. *Peter Treloar*

33

Slightly further up the line from the view on page 33, the road originally made an abrupt right-angle turn to cross the railway by a narrow bridge. This can be seen at the end of a 'tunnel' of trees in this view from 6 November 1959, the railway passing into a deep cutting on the approach to the low bridge.

To cope with the heavier traffic projected for the construction of Trawsfynedd nuclear power station, the bridge needed renewing, strengthening and the bends easing. There were initial threats to the railway, but happily these did not come to fruition and the rails remained. There was a need, however, to temporarily cross the line on the level, just behind where the photographer was standing in the first view, while the new structure was built. This view shows construction work on the new reinforced concrete bridge on 5 March 1960.

Forty years on the view looks to all intents and purposes as if it had always been this way. Nature is reclaiming and softening the surroundings by 4 May 2004 and the tall tree vies with the railway for attention. *David Rouse, MJS collection (2)/MJS*

Minffordd

Minffordd yard is a strategic part of the Ffestiniog – a place for storage, the permanent way headquarters, transhipment to and from the standard gauge (in former times) and, more recently, a superb, spacious location for special events. The former mineral line and turnout to the yard can just be discerned amongst the weeds to left of the train in this shot of *Taliesin* heading south from the station. Seen around 1959/60, driver Jim Maxwell stares grimly ahead as his short four-car train heads for Porthmadog, with a young face watching him intently from the observation car at the head of the rake. With a single dwelling visible, the whole is a very rural scene.

The slightly elevated 'past' vantage point was unavailable on 6 May 2004, but the ground-level view is just as eloquent in highlighting the railway's progress over the last half-century. On an even duller (and wetter!) day than the previous one, *Linda* accelerates her five-coach train away from the Minffordd stop, with driver Paul Davies somewhat more reticent to peer from the cab in the driving rain! His fireman watches the photographer from his dry position and a face again peers from the observation windows behind, this time a little older and from coach 101. Note the 'TTT' notice – placed as 'whistle guidance' for 'Talking Train' engine crews – on the now-bare telegraph pole; the dwelling has now had its render painted white; and the 'See us at Railfest, NRM York' headboard on Linda's tender announces the FR's intention to welcome visitors at that event later in the month. *MJS collection/MJS*

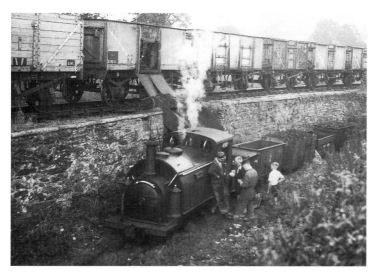

Both Minffordd yard and the adjacent standard gauge tracks were at a lower level than the FR main line. The yard was arranged to make transhipment as easy as possible with tracks at various levels, including the FR's 'coal hole' well below the standard gauge wagons. On 3 September 1958, *Prince* stands quietly simmering while the crew take a short break to discuss some matter with a visitor. The young lad concentrates his attention on the coal chute that is delivering the black stuff from a mix of BR wooden and steel wagons. Note that just three of the FR's fleet are here filled with coal and that its trackwork has not seen weedkiller for some time! *Sydney Leleux*

Around six years later, *Prince* is once again at work on shunting duties, with more mixed FR wagons, but on the level of the main yard. Driver Bill Hoole gingerly shunts his train backwards, carefully watched by his fireman, while to the left an out-of-use Ruston crane stands in front of the old goods shed, here rented out as a saw mill.

Forty years on, the goods shed, back in railway use as the Permanent Way Department workshop, has had much attention. The old derelict left-hand entrance has been converted to a roller-shutter; the roof has had transparent corrugated strips fitted, to allow light in; and a barrier has been erected to protect rail from road. But the major alteration has been in the right-hand sector of the end wall. A massive sliding door, with its own smaller entrance, has been fitted, with the original door – behind the crane in the 'past' view – blocked up. A light has also been fitted. *Tom Greaves/MJS*

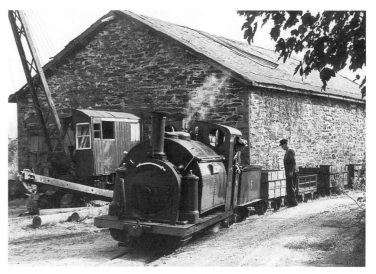

A walk from Minffordd yard to the FR station, alongside the roadway, brings the pedestrian progressively closer to the line, leading to fine photographic opportunities. In July 1977 this photographer has expertly utilised both location and summer sunshine to fashion this portrait of an immaculately turned-out *Blanche* as she slows for the station at Minffordd, nicely framed by the signal post and mature trees in the upper yard. The fireman poses for his picture, single-line token in hand, ready to jump down from the locomotive at the station, place it in the machine and obtain a fresh token for the continued run up the line. *Terry Gough*

As already mentioned, the standard gauge station at Minffordd was at a lower level than the FR. The two stations are joined by a footpath, which rises from the lower platform, behind the signal box, under the FR and up to the narrow gauge halt. This is a view from 9 May 1956 and shows *Prince*, with fireman Ann Carter, crossing the bridge. Note that the signal box is merely designated as a ground frame, controlling the access to the transhipment sidings on the extreme right. Wooden porter's trolleys, bench and oil lamp complete the period scene.

On 5 May 2004, in driving rain, suitably attired driver Paul Davies eases *David Lloyd George* away from Minffordd, nearing the end of the journey as the 1515 service from Blaenau Ffestiniog. Happily, although the transhipment siding and signal box have gone, the station is still open to passengers. The upward climb by footpath between the two stations can be seen on the left. Note the growth of trees over the period since the 'past' view and the provision of fencing to prevent access to the standard gauge from the FR's yard on the right. *H. B. Priestley, Dave Southern collection/MJS*

A 'once in a lifetime' shot – two double-headers in one portrait at Minffordd! Around 1973, two BR Sulzer Type 2s (later Class 24) – headed by No 5054, complete with route indicator discs and nose-end doors – pause with a Wirral Railway Circle special to the FR, as ex-Penrhyn Quarry 'sisters' *Linda* and *Blanche* pass over the bridge beyond. As the last of his passengers hurries up the connecting footpath, the Type 2's driver seems to be trying to make a point to his Inspector! The FR yard is to the right, without the connecting siding and yet to have the railings between the two railways put in place. *Norman Kneale*

We are now back on the FR, standing on the 'down' (ie downhill) platform at Minffordd, to witness *Prince* climbing the gradient into the station. The date is June 1957, two years after the first post-restoration passenger trains began, and the line is only open as far as Penrhyndeudraeth, the destination for this train. Note the carpeting of grass around the rails, the point control lever half buried in the undergrowth on the right, and the entrance of the footpath from the BR station, just to the left of the locomotive.

Nearly 50 years later, the motive power has improved, but the weather most certainly has not! On a wet 5 May 2004 *David Lloyd George* enters the station with the 1020 Porthmadog-Blaenau Ffestiniog train, the inclement conditions granting the photographer magnificent steam effects. Once more, driver Paul Davies peers as little as need dictates to see the road ahead, as he slows his charge for the station stop. As well as the length of train, there is much else changed over the years. Signals have appeared, together with platforms and foot crossing; a handrail now adorns the footpath between the two stations, although the previous fencing on the left has been dispensed with; more houses have been built in the right distance; and a 'Limited Clearance' sign, gradient post, lamp standard, bus stop and BR station sign have all appeared. *Peter Treloar/MJS*

As one of the few passing places on the 13-mile FR, Minffordd has its moments of frantic activity. Not least among the various actions undertaken is the exchange of tokens for the sections above and below the station. In this view from the summer of 1963, *Prince*'s fireman has his token tightly grasped as his train enters the station. To the right, *Linda* has already given up her token for the line above the station and waits for the 'right away' to deliver her load of passengers safely back in Porthmadog, including those in the First Class observation section of No 11 (again!) immediately behind her.

On 15 July 2000 an altogether more imposing vision is presented by *Earl of Merioneth* (left) passing *David Lloyd George*. Although both built by the railway's Boston Lodge Works, to the same basic Fairlie design, the outward appearance of the two is markedly different, with the *Earl* (built 1979) being far more angular in tank design than the much later (1993) and sleeker *DLG*. During January 2004 new tanks were constructed for both *Merddin Emrys* (then nearing the later stages of renewal) and the *Earl*, which will provide for this angular appearance to be consigned to history. *John Alexander, MJS collection/MJS*

While pre-war photographs at Minffordd are not exactly like the proverbial 'hen's teeth', they are certainly less common than portraits at Porthmadog; and the quality of many older views is of questionable standard. It is therefore pleasing to see this perfectly acceptable shot of *Merddin Emrys* pausing in the station on 14 August 1939. Less than a month before the outbreak of hostilities, the departing passengers, attired in summer gear, appear to be fully relaxed. Note that the guard is unlocking the coaches on the side next to the 'up' (ie uphill) track, while the fireman leans nonchalantly on his rails, awaiting the restart, with a healthy supply of coal still atop the tank in front of him.

Forty years later, on 18 September 1979, a slightly wider view shows that the restorationists have made great strides and there is much change at Minffordd. The trackwork has long been rid of weeds and more clearly ballasted; formal platforms have been installed, with lighting provided; the station's substantial hallmark tree has put on further growth; and a tall electricity pylon has sprouted to the left of the railway's boundary. *Earl of Merioneth* restarts the 1243 Tanygrisiau-Porthmadog service, with the fireman's cramped space beside the boiler here even more restricted with a second person on his side of the footplate.

Another 25 years have elapsed, and on 5 May 2004, again in rain, *David Lloyd George* arrives with the 1515 Blaenau Ffestiniog-Porthmadog service, adorned with the headboard advertising the railway's visit to the NRM later in the month. The signs and signals mentioned on page 39 are here seen from the opposite direction. The pylon is now screened by tree growth, which provides an attractive backdrop to the recently rebuilt waiting shelter on the down platform. Note that *DLG* is now back on the normal down side of the station, compared to the *Earl* above. *Robin Butterell/Tom Heavyside/MJS*

41

As has already been seen, after the 1946 abandonment of the railway nature was very quick to attempt reclamation. Seen from this low angle in June 1951, the tracks appear to have totally disappeared under the grass, and bushes and small trees are making a pitch for the platform area. Corrugated iron sheeting bars the windows of the former refreshment room on the right, and the lamps have been removed from the stanchions at both ends of the station. Otherwise, the station building looks in good shape, the curtains still at the windows providing evidence of continued occupation.

By May 2004 the nearest part of the building has been rebuilt and put to use as staff accommodation, accompanied by a flower-bed; the station now proudly displays its name; the lamps have been restored; platforms are in place and the track is now clearly visible; and notice-boards have been provided and decorated – a far healthier view! *Peter Treloar collection/MJS*

The restoration of a waiting shelter on the down platform at Minffordd, briefly mentioned on page 41, was a long-held dream of members of the railway's Heritage Group. Somewhat hampered by lack of drawings or very clear period photographs – and delayed by lack of ready funding – the new shelter was finally installed in 2003. Sadly, the original had to be demolished, being both too close to the tracks and far from safe and secure. Its decrepit state can be judged from these two views from Easter 1955. The hole to the right of the window is of interest – did it originally hold a clock, perhaps? Some clearance work is already in hand, despite the telegraph pole being devoid of wires and the track most definitely in need of TLC!

On 3 May 2004 the new building looks immaculate, its contours highlighted by the bright conditions. Restored as close as possible to the original, a side window has been added for the convenience of passengers; the surrounding area has been carefully designed and paving constructed to properly show off the building; and the filigree design of the porch support ironwork has been re-created – although the hole has not made a re-appearance! Note the number '135' to the right, part of the 'Talking Train' menu, to be accessed during a 10-minute stop here on the up journey. *Robin Butterell (2)/MJS*

Photographs of 'men at work' on the FR are, in the main, conspicuous by their absence – mostly due to the need for the railway to operate at times convenient to visitors – so it is pleasing to have this shot of work being undertaken on the track at Minffordd. On 10 October 1962, after the close of the summer season, the workers take a well-earned tea – and smoke! – break during track relaying in the up platform. Sleepers and rails lie scattered, awaiting re-use, and there is evidence of some sawing having taken place. Note the tracks converging at the far end of the platform for the single-line to run northwards over Gwyndy Bank.

A year later, another season has ended and permanent way work is again under way. This time *Linda*, newly arrived from Penrhyn Quarry the previous year, heads a train of 'long-welded rail' northwards, bound for Highgate in October 1963. While three of the party enjoy a footplate ride, the two on the veranda of the brake-van appear to be enjoying having their portrait taken, with Ron Lester (PW foreman, left) sporting a very wide grin! Note the rather optimistic 'Change for Great Western Railways' addendum to the station nameboard!

On 5 May 2004 the ancient tree still dominates the scene as the 1600 Porthmadog-Blaenau Ffestiniog service departs, with Observation Car No 101 trailing. The guard peers from his doorway, ensuring that there are no last-minute hitches.
David Rouse, MJS collection/John Alexander, MJS collection/MJS

Beyond the tree and looking back towards Boston Lodge, *Linda*, now oil-fired, is captured slowing for the stop at Minffordd at the head of the 0930 Porthmadog-Tanygrisiau train on 29 May 1979. The late-spring sunshine beautifully illuminates both the general view and the arboreal splendour on the right. Without doubt, early morning is the best time to record both station and trains at this location.

Twenty-five years later not much has changed, in comparison to other parts of the railway. *Linda* is seen again on 6 May 2004, arriving as the 1020 Porthmadog-Blaenau Ffestiniog service, but in distinctly duller weather conditions and temporarily fitted with a tender cab cover, to enhance the crew's comfort. The platforms are now graced with seats and floral decoration, and the station nameboard has been removed from the tree trunk and placed on its own supporting posts. Elsewhere, the increased tree canopy gives a less open feel than of yore. *Tom Heavyside/MJS*

In this view from beside the down line in 1968, that year's FR Society AGM gives us a glimpse of a very much rarer sight – two trains apparently heading in the same direction! To the left, *Earl of Merioneth* heads a service train into the station, past *Blanche* waiting to take AGM members, many of whom have arrived by standard gauge, further up the line. Note that at this stage the down platform has not been extended to match the length of its neighbour.

As was seen on page 17, the introduction of the 'Talking Train' was a major innovation on the FR in 2004 – the first product of this nature on a railway anywhere in the world! Giving the travelling public a wholly new experience as they travel up the line, the individual handsets – entrusted to the passengers as part of the package – provide appropriately detailed, fascinating and even intriguing information relevant to the locations on the trip. A 10-minute stop is allowed at Minffordd for participants to explore the location and to learn of its various features. On Good Friday, the day before the public launch, one of the final trial trips pauses at the station, with *Prince* at the head of vintage stock and suitably adorned with headboard. Note that platforms are now the order of the day on both sides of the tracks. *Howard Wilson/MJS*

While many hundreds of photographers annually snap away on the stations or at well-known locations, a few more adventurous among them try for that more special shot. By walking beyond the station confines, this photographer has delightfully manipulated both train and sun direction to create a most pleasing vista. On 29 May 1979 *Mountaineer* – in near-original FR condition – accelerates away from the Minffordd stop with the 1000 Porthmadog-Tanygrisiau train. Note how bare is the trackside at this point, following winter relaying and the lateness of the background trees coming into leaf. *Tom Heavyside*

Half a mile or so further on *Mountaineer* is again portrayed, but this time some five years later and altered to a Fairlie-style cab design, climbing Gwyndy Bank on 9 September 1984 and now bound for Blaenau Ffestiniog, following the opening to that destination two years earlier. Again the photographer has thoughtfully employed location, landscape and foliage to create this pleasing portrait – an example to us all! *Tom Heavyside*

Penrhyndeudraeth

Between Gwyndy and the station at Penrhyndeudraeth, the railway runs through very pleasant, undulating countryside. After a fairly straight run from Gwyndy, the line swings right round Ty Fry curve, and approaching the entrance to the curve in June 1957 is *Prince*, close to his destination at Penrhyndeudraeth. The undulating nature of the scenery is well seen on either side of the line, while a low stone wall acts as the railway's boundary. Note the rather ancient-looking telegraph pole with just a single strand!

Slightly further into the curve on the same day, Will Jones is hard at work with a spot of re-sleepering. Despite the relatively lightweight track, he still needs to put his back into the exercise!

Even further around the bend, approaching the site of Pen-y-Bryn Halt later on the same day, Will Jones and his assistant, Evie Roberts, stand aside as *Prince* brings another up train towards Penrhyn, the driver carefully monitoring the position of the two men. With the assistant's jacket laid out on the ground, it was obviously warm work on this summer's day, despite the dull conditions. *All Peter Treloar*

The first of these three views of Penrhyn station, as approached from the south, is undated, but with the main line through the station totally obliterated by grass and no sign of it in the roadway in the foreground, with only the very short spur into the yard visible, this is after closure in 1946 and probably around 1949/50. The area appears undisturbed by human attention and is, to all intents and purposes, asleep, though the local Co-op still used the corrugated buildings beyond the stone goods shed.

After gaining possession of the railway in 1954, the restorationists made good their relentless progress northwards by re-opening Penrhyn station to the travelling public on 20 April 1957. Many early services were handled by *Prince* – as already seen – and he is seen running round the coaching stock – stabled on a newly installed loop line – to become the 2.30pm return service to Porthmadog on 2 August 1957. 'Firewoman' Ann Carter works the point lever, no doubt appreciating the warmth of the summer sunshine.

The third photograph is also undated – but probably around 1958 – and shows two young ladies making conversation with *Taliesin*'s fireman during the stop at the station. Heads peer from the train, wondering what is happening! *Peter Treloar collection/ H. B. Priestley, Peter Treloar collection/David Lawrence, Hugh Davies collection*

Although undisturbed by unwanted human attention during its post-1946 'sleep', the station building at Penrhyn could not escape the ravages of the weather in this part of North Wales. This 8 January 1955 view shows some of the challenge ahead for those intrepid souls keen to restore infrastructure as well as services.

Another moment captured for posterity by this photographer in June 1957 shows *Prince* – with a decidedly empty tender! – waiting to return to Porthmadog. As seen in this elevated view, the dilapidated end of the building seen above has been removed; corrugated iron sheeting acts as a temporary protection; there are seats and posters for waiting passengers to enjoy; and the area looks far tidier than two years earlier. Though basically sound, the roof has not yet received attention.

After re-openings further up the line, the need for a passing loop at Penrhyn disappeared and the line on which *Prince* stood in 1957 was removed. As seen on a very dull 5 May 2004, the station building is now in a much healthier state and the whole ambience of the area is one of peaceful relaxation enlivened by the attractive flowerbeds. As the sign declares, the building now acts as a volunteer hostel, and traffic from this and incoming tourists adds to the local economy. *Bob Smallman/Peter Treloar/MJS*

Another shot from the January 1955 visit by this photographer shows the station building from the other, northerly end. The extent of reclamation by natural forces is clear, as is the abandoned air. Note the three tall, attractively topped chimneys, the route of the running line lost beneath the undergrowth, and what appears to be a blocked-up window space in the near end wall.

Yet another view from June 1957 again shows the transformation over the two years since the previous picture. *Prince* stands in the loop line at the head of the train from Porthmadog, immediately prior to running round for the return trip.

More than three decades later the railway is now open all the way to Blaenau Ffestiniog. On 21 October 1989 *Mountaineer* slows for a brief stop with a late-season 0945 service from Porthmadog. Alongside the trackbed the Parks & Gardens Department are actively engaged in laying the new platform blocks, to further enhance the aesthetics of the area, which have already had a helping hand from recent paintwork on the hostel building. *Bob Smallman/ Peter Treloar (2)*

The real thing! In normal, everyday service in the inter-war years, *Merddin Emrys* slowly enters Penrhyn in July 1936 with an up train. The flat-capped fireman smiles to have his portrait taken.

Despite the innocuous appearance, this is a much rarer photograph. On Monday 12 November 1956, K. W. C. Grand – General Manager of BR (WR) – and his entourage paid a visit to the railway. Over the preceding weekend, in preparation, Allan Garraway and others laboured, fettling and clearing the track to Penrhyn, with a 'trial run' undertaken on the Sunday afternoon. This view shows that run having reached Penrhyn, on 11 November, with local youngsters intrigued at the sight and *Taliesin* blowing off prior to the return.

A slightly wider angle shows the transformation over the past five decades. In equally inclement conditions, *David Lloyd George* steams into Penrhyn on 5 May 2004 as the 1340 Porthmadog-Blaenau Ffestiniog train. Note the lighting now fitted to the hostel building and the completed platform, all adding to its aesthetics. *HB Tours, Martin Cook collection/Bob Smallman/MJS*

On its journey from the valley floor, the road from Penrhyn to Beddgelert climbs up to, then passes over, the railway by a level crossing. The gathering line of cars in the foreground indicates that the gates of the crossing are here closed to road traffic. On an unspecified day in May 1960, *Taliesin* sends attractive smoke signals as it accelerates away from the Penrhyn stop towards the crossing, with a Porthmadog-Tan-y-bwlch train; unusually, there are two crew members on the fireman's side of the double boiler. The short-trousered lad on the wall (left) seems more interested in the photographer than the train!

Apart from the more modern designs of motor vehicle, the basic view is incredibly little changed over the succeeding 44 years, with the 1993-vintage *David Lloyd George* bearing the familiar Double-Fairlie family shape and the coaches being an almost identical rake. On 5 May 2004, acceleration is again the order of the day as *DLG* lifts its load up the rising gradient towards the crossing forming the 1340 Porthmadog-Blaenau Ffestiniog service. Apart from only one occupant of the fireman's domain on this occasion, the only real change is the appearance of a bungalow on the hilltop above the loco. *Derek Cross, Peter Treloar collection/MJS*

For our first view of the actual crossing, we have another scene from the days before passengers could ride this far. On the evening of 28 May 1955, after yet another day of toil and sweat by the illustrious volunteers and with Allan Garraway as driver, some of their number enjoy the excitement and uncertainty of a ride on or behind the Simplex *Mary Anne*! Judging by the body language of the various individuals, it rather looks as though *Mary* is not being wholly co-operative!

Taking a slightly wider view of the same location on 8 May 1995, *David Lloyd George* is again seen at Penrhyn, this time with an early 0815 Porthmadog-Blaenau Ffestiniog train, which seems to have trapped walker and dog in 'no man's land' during their constitutional! Under normal circumstances, being between the gates shown and those controlling the traffic from the Beddgelert direction – behind the photographer – is totally *verboten*!

Fast forward nine years, and May Day 2004 sees an unusual 'early bird', the 0815 Boston Lodge-Dduallt slate train. Such was the unusual hour at this location that Hilary Davies, at precisely 0837, very nearly missed giving husband Paul his 'snap' (lunch)! The look on Paul's face gives expression to his anxiety! As part of the Bank Holiday 'Interactive' weekend, *Prince* gathers speed northwards with a healthy consist of slate wagons, 'passengers' and brakesmen, ready to give participants a 'white-knuckle' ride on the return! *Bob Smallman/MJS (2)*

Turning through 180 degrees, the view north during the closure years is one of gradual decline and dereliction and certainly not one to encourage thoughts of restoration. Taken in the very early days of the railway being in the restorationists' hands, on 27 October 1954, this was a scene that convinced the progenitors of the proposed hydro-electric scheme at Tanygrisiau that the railway would never again run trains over this crossing. Note the white house standing proud on the hill on the left, later to become Talgarth, a B&B run by railway supporters and volunteers Paul and Hilary Davies.

How wrong they were! It doesn't pay to underestimate the British 'Bulldog Spirit' nor the grit and determination when enthusiasts sink their teeth into a project! From 5 April 1958 – less than 3½ years after the 'past' view – trains were once again running past this point to Tan-y-bwlch and, during the season, they were crossing this roadway several times a day. This is the view on 19 September 1995, during a quiet period, with the road having 'right of way'. Note that the tree growth has hidden the Davies's retreat. *Central Electric Authority/MJS*

On 1 September 1957 *Prince* makes his way back down the line with a mixed rake of permanent way wagons. Not yet open to the public, work was progressing as swiftly as possible further up the line, with the goal of re-opening to Tan-y-bwlch, and this was a train returning down the line, the rostered day's work completed.

Eight years later, in the summer of 1965, Tan-y-bwlch has become a very popular destination. Now on passenger duties, *Prince* once again runs downhill with a returning service train to Porthmadog, driver and fireman both watching the way ahead and the four coaches bearing a very healthy number of happy visitors. *Brian Pask/Terry Gough*

With the very tight curves on many parts of the route and the extremely limited clearances, images such as this – a southbound train from the valley side – can only be obtained from the carriage window with a very long lens. This vantage point has been very well handled by the photographer, capturing *Merddin Emrys* crossing the road during the railway's centenary celebrations, in August 1963. A family stands outside the end terrace to enjoy the spectacle.

A longer lens has also been chosen for this comparison. Standing slightly further back, the photographer has captured *David Lloyd George* attacking the climb from the station stop, with attractive pictorial effects arising from the 'contra-jour' approach. The date is 5 August 1995 and the train is the 1455 Porthmadog-Blaenau Ffestiniog, whose exhaust is virtually lost in the heat. *Jon Marsh/MJS*

With a constant downhill gradient from Blaenau Ffestiniog, every train up from Porthmadog has a constant slog. There are shifts in actual gradient over the route, but the climb is not quite as draconian as appears from this portrait of *Merddin Emrys* on the run from Penrhyn to Rhiw Goch. At the head of the 1115 up train, *Merddin Emrys* shows signs of the hard work required, however, especially with a heavy load, as he lifts his train upwards on 8 September 1972. *Geoff King*

Rhiw Goch to Plas Halt

Mention has already been made of the heroic efforts of volunteers – well, here's a picture of some of them in action! During the summer of 1957, as part of the 'push' to re-open to Tan-y-bwlch, a group of (at least ten) hackers, snippers and pullers attack the undergrowth on the southern approach to Rhiw Goch, watched in the distance by a gently simmering *Prince*. Who were they, and where are they now? We have already travelled 3 miles from Boston Lodge, but we are still only half way to Tan-y-bwlch, so there's another 3 miles of bushwhacking ahead for this crowd!

Three decades later, the story is so different. The 'past' location is beyond the far end of the train, which steams past the now cleared site at Rhiw Goch on 19 April 1986 behind the two 'Ladies', *Linda* leading *Blanche* on the 1220 Porthmadog-Blaenau Ffestiniog turn. The railway has climbed 225 feet in the 3 miles from sea level at Boston Lodge, and with that same distance to go to Tan-y-bwlch, Rhiw Goch is an ideal location for a passing loop and a refuge siding. The headboard proudly proclaims 'The World's Oldest Independent Railway' – a truism then in its 150th year and still so today. Note the 'modern' colour light signalling installed here. *MJS collection/Hugh Ballantyne*

In this view of the refuge siding in use, it is occupied by a very special visitor. On 1 May 1988, during a visit to the FR, ex-WHR loco *Russell* makes an historic trip to this point, something that would not have been possible in as-built 1906 condition, due to FR gauge restrictions. Even after the WHR ran into the FR's Harbour station in Porthmadog after 1923, *Russell* only ever reached these dizzy heights once. While they wait for the road to return downhill, the assembled group are no doubt aware of this – especially as the late-lamented FR archivist Michael Seymour is one of their number – and are enjoying their part in the momentous occasion. *Peter Treloar*

Turning through 180 degrees to look north, we have another unusual sight. With the constant gradient and the twists and turns on the route ahead to Tan-y-bwlch, trains are normally scheduled and signalled to run straight past Rhiw Goch on the upwards journey. On this unidentified date, however, *Linda* has been stopped at the signals – most likely due to a late-running down train, but one that has already departed from Tan-y-bwlch. Driver Arthur Brooks attends to his charge, while his unidentified fireman watches for signs of the offending train. *Tom Greaves*

Our final look at Rhiw Goch is of a Parks & Gardens Dept train about to be shunted in the refuge siding by *Prince*, for the volunteers to have a spot of lunch before continuing their afternoon labours. Note 'generalissimo' Gordon Rushton – then General Manager of the railway – in the white cap. Judging by hats and coats liberally scattered among participants, the weather is none too kind on 22 October 1989. *Peter Treloar*

Due to the topography of the route down from Blaenau Ffestiniog, the railway is graced with a number of impressive structures. Not least among these is Cei Mawr (Great Quay in English), a 62-foot-high dry-stone embankment describing a long right-hand curve shortly after leaving Rhiw Goch. Originally built for the railway's opening in 1836, it received major attention in 1887-89, then stood 'untouched' for a century, until the present railway again gave it some further attention in 1989. It still serves the railway today largely as it did on day one – a tribute to the navvies who first created the line. Some of the magnificence can be judged from this scene of an up train, taken in July 1936.

A slightly wider camera angle, from further back on a train, again demonstrates the size and awesome nature of Cei Mawr, manfully supporting the much heavier trains than originally envisaged. On 21 August 1991, *Merddin Emrys* heads an 11-coach formation across the embankment, as the 1325 Porthmadog-Blaenau Ffestiniog service. The open views formerly enjoyed here and at other locations along the line have become veiled by tree growth over recent years, leading to customer complaints and the railway planning remedial action. *HB Tours, Martin Cook collection/Peter Treloar*

One thing that the railway enjoys – and does with skill and style – is having fun. It realises that as well as providing a professional service to the travelling public, its visitors also derive much pleasure from indulging in some lighter moments. A re-creation of the old gravity slate trains has already been seen; most travel up the line as a separate entity, whereas in early days wagons would be added to the rear of passenger workings. Thus, on 30 September 1995, the 1250 Porthmadog departure provides a re-creation of this mode of working, captured as the incredibly long train passes over Cei Mawr, with the wagons empty of slate, as they would have been in the early days. Heads out of the windows indicate that the arrangement is certainly creating much interest. *Peter Treloar*

63

Left Shortly before reaching Plas Halt, the railway passes above Plas Tan-y-bwlch, once the palatial home of William Oakley, owner of one of the most successful slate mines at Blaenau Ffestiniog, but now base for the Snowdonia National Park Environmental Studies Centre. Rounding a curve above the southern end of the house's grounds on 18 October 1986, *Blanche* shows evidence of her hard work in lifting the 1220 Porthmadog-Blaenau Ffestiniog up and around this tortuous stretch. *Peter Treloar*

Below Two years earlier and slightly closer to Plas Halt, *Blanche* is again seen driving northwards with the 1220 Porthmadog departure. On this date, while passengers on this train enjoy both ride and views, a railway convention was being held below in Plas Tan-y-bwlch. *Peter Treloar*

The final approach to Plas Halt – by rail and foot! The delightful wicket gate on the left doubles as protection from the trains and access to the footpath down to Plas Tan-y-bwlch from the station site (behind the photographer). An 'unofficial' halt on the original railway, for the sole use of the Oakley family and their guests, was nearby – just up the line from the lower view opposite – but a more formal structure was established at this new location in June 1963 by the restorationists, to accompany the opening up of the house to visitors and to encourage some of them to use the railway. A request stop, its usage has not found total favour among train crews, as on up trains they then have the problem of restarting on the rising gradient on often damp rails, with over a mile of twisting track to negotiate before reaching Tan-y-bwlch. In July 1972 there are stern faces on *Linda*'s footplate as this train prepares to stop. *Terry Gough*

Close to Plas halt, the permanent way gang used the body of an extremely elderly quarrymen's coach as a line hut. *Linda* races past the structure during the summer of 1966, once more with Allan Garraway at the controls. *Mike Mensing*

Half a mile further on, the railway rounds Whistling Curve, so named as up trains whistled here to signal to Tan-y-bwlch station of their approach. In an undated view around 1965, *Earl of Merioneth* (originally named *Livingston Thompson* and now in the NRM, York) – with Evan Davies at the helm – blankets the forest with smoke and steam as it rounds the curve on a train from Porthmadog. *Adrian Vaughan collection, Percy Pike collection*

In another view of the location, *Linda* runs tender-first downhill in the summer of 1966, past the then very open avenue between the trees. A short-sleeved Allan Garraway, in casual stance, keeps his eye on the road ahead. This view is now impossible due to the growth of trees over the past 40 years. The summer sunshine has obviously brought out the tourists, judging by the healthy number of passengers on board, and no doubt the crew appreciate the warm and dry conditions. *Mike Mensing*

Tan-y-bwlch

At a little over half way from Porthmadog, Tan-y-bwlch has always been an important staging post, for both trains and people. At 430 feet above sea level, it is also just over half the climb to the summit of the line at its terminus at Blaenau Ffestiniog. When opened in July 1873 – to replace the horse staging place (1836-63), then the passenger station (1865-73) at nearby Hafod-y-Llyn – Tan-y-bwlch was a very open site, with views through virtually 360 degrees. This view from the 1880s demonstrates this openness, with Creuau embankment – where William Oakley laid the first stone for the railway in February 1833 – beyond the station, and the line up to Garnedd in the distance. The FR's second Double-Fairlie, *James Spooner*, heads a down train on the left, whilst *Merddin Emrys*, built by the FR itself in 1879, takes water before restarting his mixed train towards Blaenau Ffestiniog. Sadly, forestation over the ensuing 100-plus years has destroyed this delightful vista. *F. Frith, FR archives*

The final entry to Tan-y-bwlch from the south is by way of a bridge over a narrow road, then a straight run through a shallow cutting. Emerging from the latter on 13 June 1959, *Prince* arrives with the 2.30pm service from Porthmadog. The remains of the original goods loop are still in situ on the left. Evidence of recent track work – a pile of rail chairs, spikes, etc, lying on the ground to the left of the train – is the result of moving the set of points to beneath the locomotive, to shorten the loop. The fireman looks down disconsolately at this debris.

A comparative view on 9 April 2004 shows *Prince* still in regular use, this time making an energetic departure

from the station at precisely 1543, with the returning 'Talking Train', its participants having enjoyed a lunchtime/early afternoon sojourn at the stop, sampling the café's wares and the delights of passing trains. *Prince* now has a red livery, compared to the old all-over green, and far more aesthetically pleasing curves on the running plate. Note the old siding area, now replaced by a child's play area bounded by the white fencing; and the growth of bushes and trees on the far embankment. *Gerald Adams/MJS*

Looking north from near to the end of the old loop, 25 June 1963 is another wet day! With Wellington boots, sou'westers and raingear the order of the day, a young child runs towards *Merddin Emrys*, which is making plenty of smoke and steam in the conditions as he runs round his train, out of sight to the left. The tall nameboard leaves no doubt as to where we are, with the old goods shed just beyond.

Conscious of 'health and safety' long before it became an over-riding preoccupation in our society, the FR not only built a formal platform at Tan-y-bwlch but also erected fencing, to protect both people and cars from the running lines. The goods shed has been turned into a café, and, more recently, a protective awning has been attached for the benefit of diners or those who just want to watch trains. This is the deserted view at 1235 on a damp 4 May 2004, between services and with diners well ensconced inside the café! Note the substantial footbridge that has provided access to the platforms since the early 1970s. *MJS collection/MJS*

The reverse of the nameboard seen on the previous page can be seen here, to the right of the old goods shed, which still has its track and siding in this view from January 1959. Also visible on the left are the remains of coal chutes, but the wooden crane that once stood in front of the shed is long gone. The bare winter trees allow a view of the hills beyond.

In the second picture it is the winter of 1965/66, the station has been open again to passengers for around eight years, and, during these winter months, the goods shed is being converted into a café. The basic outline of the building remains, but windows are being installed to greatly enhance the dining ambience. The background trees are still permitting views at this time of year.

The transformation complete, picnic tables have replaced the coal chutes; posters adorn the entrance beside the double doorway; the yard tracks have been removed and tarmac has replaced grass and sidings, to hold more tables, some under the awning; and the trees now do their best to shield the view beyond. The station is still a popular stopping-off point for local walkers as well as rail travellers, but the weather of 4 May 2004 is unlikely to encourage sale of either the advertised film or ice-cream! *MJS collection/Howard Wilson/MJS*

In early restoration days, with original trackwork still in place, this is a rare photograph of the figure pictured marching towards the camera in determined style, thought to be Len Heath-Humphrys, instigator of the movement that eventually became the FR Society, and without whom we would not have the railway we know today. The photograph is undated, but probably shows the 1958 FRS AGM train, which had run to Tan-y-bwlch for the first time. In the distance *Taliesin* attracts attention from members, both on the ground and on the very bare cutting sides, as it runs round its train.

Over the next decade the priority was consolidation. In peak periods, traffic was greatly exceeding the capacity of the rolling-stock, locos and – above all – the track! There was considerable pressure to forge on to Dduallt, but Allan Garraway sought to ensure that sense prevailed, pointing out the dangers and that he could not be held responsible if the railway overstretched itself. At Tan-y-bwlch, this consolidation included the provision of a footbridge to cross the line and give access to the new platforms, built over the winter of 1970/71. Viewed from this useful vantage point, *Mountaineer* climbs the last few yards into the station on 6

September 1972, leaving the cutting that is now populated by a variety of flora that prevents the previous photographic opportunities. Note that, in addition to the realignment of the track and the presence of point rodding alongside, fencing has been installed alongside the café, which is out of the picture to the left.

A further three decades have seen yet more change and development – in both motive power and type of train as well as with the infrastructure. On 3 May 2004 Single-Fairlie *Taliesin*, built at Boston Lodge in 1999, arrives at the station with the 1500 Porthmadog-Tan-y-bwlch 'Talking Train' service. Note that, in addition to yet more prodigious growth on either side of the cutting, the siding to the left of the running line has been removed, allowing the fencing to be extended to incorporate a small play area for children young and old. The point rodding and mechanisms seen in 1972 have now been replaced by electronic control, with wiring buried in trunking. *Bob Smallman/Geoff King/MJS*

A 180-degree turn shows the view from the footbridge looking towards Blaenau. Since the provision of the island platform and the extensions towards Blaenau Ffestiniog, down trains more usually run into the left-hand face, but in April 1972 the station was temporarily not a crossing place, so *Merddin Emrys* is not defying the rules as he restarts the day's 'Festiniog Railway Special', for the FRS AGM, from the up platform. Note the provision of clocks to give the times of the next trains up and down the line – by 1975 these had disappeared, although most other platform furniture remained. Within a couple of years of this view, point rodding would snake between the up track and the wooden fencing.

By May 2004 the platforms are no longer openly designated as '1' or '2', but are now signposted for the direction of the trains: in this view, for Porthmadog (left) and for the top of the line at Blaenau Ffestiniog (right). Lighting has now been provided, but otherwise little has changed on the platforms. *Taliesin* slows for the stop

with the 'Talking Train' seen arriving on page 71, properly using the up track. As in so many other facets of its operation, the FR has kept up to date with development in motive power, introducing modern diesels to the line, but it also produced in the late 1990s this re-creation of Single-Fairlie No 7 of 1876, a type long disappeared from the railway but which was a common sight in the early years of the 20th century. *Dave Southern/ MJS*

Here is a picture that truly deserves to have a page to itself! In more relaxed days, when waiting passengers could approach the train without hindrance and the hills beyond were still visible as a magnificent backdrop. *Taliesin* opens up to begin the return journey to Porthmadog on 18 May 1959. Fireman John Brisley poses for his portrait, ignoring the two or three other photographers, while in the background Bessie Jones, resplendent in her Welsh costume, chats to a visitor. Note the carpet of daisies between the tracks to the right of the train. *Peter Gray*

Bessie is again seen here, this time sharing a joke with *Prince*'s fireman in the moments before the return journey to Porthmadog in October 1958. The 'right away' is not imminent, however, as coach doors stand open to welcome travellers. The sign advertises that 'Teas' are available at the station house – courtesy of Bessie – and other refreshments, tickets and guidebooks are available from the Buffet Car on the train. The guard stands in his doorway, solicitous to the needs of the two ladies.

Four years later, the season is obviously not yet over, with a longer train to cope with the increased patronage on 13 September 1962. *Earl of Merioneth* gently simmers in the late-summer sunshine, again with doors open, while the assembled throng enjoy both warmth and view. Note the station house to the left, from where Bessie dispensed her teas, and the large rock sprouting from the ground – protecting the point lever from unwary car drivers but a hazard to the unwary pedestrian – and a must for removal as the railway redesigned the station area.

The present situation at Tan-y-bwlch has a much less relaxed atmosphere, with cars and people segregated from the tracks by the fencing. Such has been the growth of traffic over the years, on top of the current preoccupation with 'health and safety', that this precaution cannot be avoided. In some senses the station is 'boom or bust', in that there are busy times when two trains share the island platform interspersed with periods of peace and tranquillity. The former is here seen on 4 May 2004, but without many people actually on the platform, as the up train on the right is leaving and the down one prepares for departure. Note the installation of an original-style FR signal, to re-create the structure that once controlled trains in the station area, and the 1873 booking office on the right, still in daily use, but now for S&T purposes. *Mike Esau/Bryan Hicks/MJS*

In the first of these three views looking south from the platform area, the open nature of the site can still be savoured in this view of *Merddin Emrys* waiting to return to Porthmadog. On 25 June 1963 the driver of the 3.25pm departure slowly approaches his charge carrying his oil feeder, having tended to his routine duties. Just visible between him and the goods shed on the right, the coal chutes remain in situ.

The date of the second picture is Thursday 10 July 1969, and the extension to Dduallt has been brought into use. With a train for this further destination, *Blanche* rounds the recently installed island platform with an afternoon departure from Porthmadog, the driver checking on the position (and motive?) of the photographer. Note that the up destination board now boasts the availability of a run to Dduallt and that temporary wire fencing now guards the tracks, pending the provision of a more attractive permanent wooden feature. A porter's trolley adds an attractive feature, bottom right.

During a quiet period – the lull before the storm! – the station gently snoozes, with station furniture now comprising seating, lighting, flower tubs and destination boards. The view beyond to the hills in May 2004 is now restricted both by fencing and the continuing growth of surrounding trees. The old goods shed, now converted to a fine café and bookshop, is lost behind the footbridge in this view. *Alan Ashworth, MJS collection/Horace Gamble/MJS*

Left In a view that is no longer possible, the photographer has taken advantage of his work felling trees in August 1966 – to make space for a siding – to capture this view from the top of a ladder and a tree! Though it was unusual to have two full-length trains at Tan-y-bwlch at this time, high summer traffic sometimes required extra trains – just look at those cars! With obviously warm temperatures, passengers are relaxed in their enjoyment of the surroundings, and on the right a small knot of them take advantage of Bessie Jones's teas and ices. *Howard Wilson*

The railway is still three years away from restoring traffic to the site and is in somnolent state as captured by the photographer in August 1955. Closed to passengers on 15 September 1939, following the outbreak of war, only Will Jones's sheep and Bessie's chickens have prevented nature from taking a complete hold on the station! The water tower and station house rest in the solitude, with smoke drifting lazily from a chimney of the latter.

The base of the water tower and the station house are still extant, but in May 2004 the former is now without its tank, replaced by the larger structure beyond, and the house is now in private occupation, separated from the railway by the fencing clearly seen around it. Note how the trackwork has been redesigned in conjunction with the provision of the island platform, and that a colour light signal and warning sign have sprouted between the tracks. A permanent way/engineer's train prepares to depart at 1225, to run south between timetabled services. Note the clearance of the trees on the right, as mentioned opposite. *Bob Smallman/MJS*

The tree clearance already mentioned and the new siding are more clearly portrayed from this angle, at the top end of the station complex on 1 June 1966. *Linda* pauses for water and attention – from both crew and public – before running round, while passengers are enjoying either a casual stroll around the site or a picnic in the far field.

The new siding was laid to facilitate works trains to and from Dduallt during construction of the Deviation. With this long complete – and the loss of sidings at the bottom end of the station – a re-arrangement provided a pair here at the top end. It is a tight fit but there is still a path beyond them and a picnic in the field is still possible – weather permitting! *H. B. Priestley, Peter Treloar collection/MJS*

Immediately north of Tan-y-bwlch, the railway runs on to the narrow Creuau Bank, site of the laying of the foundation stone in 1833. A sight that is not normally experienced by present-day enthusiasts or photographers is here seen on 6 September 1972, with *Merddin Emrys*, bottom-end working hard, accelerating across the Bank with the 1115 Porthmadog-Dduallt service. Note that this is the 1970-model *Merddin*, the usual smooth Double-Fairlie lines lost to a rebuilding with a D-shaped smokebox saddle, parallel boiler, square tanks and open cab sides. The redesign was certainly not a visual success and, happily, the loco was to regain his true style some years later. The rather precipitous nature of the terrain is well displayed in this view. *Geoff King*

Above Leaving Creuau Bank, the railway climbs towards Garnedd Tunnel on a shelf along the hillside, with the valley floor way below to the right. This view from 21 August 1961 amply demonstrates the problems faced by the railway's construction gangs in the 1830s, and is testament to their skills and perseverance. At this time the services were still restricted to Tan-y-bwlch, leaving the trackbed open to interested enthusiasts and walkers to explore. *Sydney Leleux*

Middle Almost up to the mouth of the tunnel in July 1977, *Merddin Emrys*, still in his 'ugly suit' and lacking his top-end dome cover, gets to grips with the climb and the crew prepare to experience the blanket of smoke within the tunnel. Note how much cleaner the trackbed, walls and fencing look after the ministrations of an exercise by an Army Railway Operating Company in 1965/66. *Terry Gough*

Bottom We go back in time for this close-up of the tunnel mouth: on 23 April 1957 the grass is claiming possession and water lies beside the track within the tunnel, while a solitary explorer is at the far end. Note the severely restricted clearances – both height and width – of the tunnel, as it bores through the outcrop of hard rock, and the shelf to the right that carried the tracks when the railway was first built. This path is now blocked by a rudimentary fence, which continues over the outcrop. *Brian Pask*

At the other end of the tunnel, in the spring of 1964, *Linda* emerges into Garnedd East, but not as a service train, as Dduallt is still four years away. Having come to the FR from Penrhyn Quarry in the summer of 1962, *Linda* was out of gauge for structures such as Garnedd, so over the winter of 1963/64 she was cut down to size and this portrait is of her and coach No 14 – ex-Lynton & Barnstaple and also rebuilt to fit the FR – on a trial run to check clearance through the tunnel.

A decade later, on 29 May 1974, services are through to Dduallt, the trackbed is now in fine shape, and *Mountaineer* bursts from the tunnel with the 1020 Porthmadog-Dduallt service. Arriving on the FR in 1967, again out of gauge, *Mountaineer* is here in the interim state of merely having its cab reduced in height and width. Later there would be more radical alterations that would dramatically alter its appearance. *MJS collection/John Scrace, Peter Johnson collection*

On to Dduallt

Set above Dduallt Manor, Campbell's Platform is the next passenger facility, some 1½ miles above Tan-y-bwlch, but only operating as a request stop. It is approached around a long sweeping right-hand bend known colloquially as 'Tank Curve' after a water tank that stands by the lineside. In the first of two views from 24 August 1985, 1979-vintage *Earl of Merioneth* enters the shallow embankment curve with its ten-coach train, operating as the 1125 departure from Porthmadog. Judging by the number of faces at windows, the load will be heavy for the Double-Fairlie to lift up the gradient.

Following the alignment and now looking up the line, the eponymous tank can just be discerned lurking behind the second coach of the train, which will cross the one in the view above at Tan-y-bwlch. Motive power this time is *Merddin Emrys*, a century older than its 'twin' above, having been built by the original FR but here in its 1970 bastardised form. With only eight coaches present here, the train is the 1155 return roster from Blaenau Ffestiniog. The site of Campbell's Platform is just off the picture to the right, while the embankment buttress, below the coaches, is common to both views. *Both Hugh Ballantyne*

The private siding at Campbell's Platform was established both for the benefit of Colonel Campbell – the owner of Dduallt Manor, below the line on the right – and the 'Deviationists', who set up a Mess in one of his barns. The trolley in the foreground is theirs, used to carry luggage and supplies, such as the stove from Tan-y-bwlch when they came to work. The little Simplex loco belonged to the Colonel and was his private transport to and from Tan-y-bwlch, for years the nearest road access to the Manor. The halt remains but, following the building of a road to the Manor and re-opening to Blaenau Ffestiniog, the operationally awkward siding has been removed.

The comparative view in the bright spring sunshine of 3 May 2004 shows just how well the site of the siding has been disguised by subsequent landscaping. The tiny waiting shelter stands on the left, while the tank is still extant but hiding behind the telegraph pole at the entrance to the curve. With the halt being request only – and at the top of a steep climb from the footpath by Dduallt Manor – it is truly a place of peace and tranquillity. *Howard Wilson/MJS*

These two views looking north show change and progress. In the first, during its 'siding years', the request nature of the halt is well exemplified, with a very determined arm outstretched to signal that *Merddin Emrys* is required to stop on his return journey from Dduallt on 2 August 1973. The flared trousers – complete with 'designer' patch – are from the period, as is the quilted jacket of the younger man! Note the rudimentary waiting seat on the platform and the 'Limited Clearance' sign on the extreme left.

By 1 June 1989 the siding has long gone, a proper seat has been installed – sited to view the glorious expanse across the valley – a floral tub is in place and the station name now adorns the waiting shelter, with another nameboard now located behind the photographer. The 1215 down train from Blaenau Ffestiniog, hauled by *Merddin Emrys*, slows to answer another request, this time from the photographer himself! *Sydney Leleux/Peter Treloar*

We are now on the final approaches to Dduallt from the south. The station's home signal repeater is seen to the right of *Linda*'s tender as she descends the gradient from the pause at the isolated location with the 1448 return train to Porthmadog on 6 September 1972. The visitors in Observation Car No 100 are hopefully appreciating the magnificent views to the far hills, and unaware that the crew of the loco – and the two 'guests' on the footplate – seem to be more focused on conversation than the track ahead of them! *Geoff King*

The area around Dduallt is very marshy in places, as can be seen to the right of the trackbed as *Mountaineer*, still in early FR style, heads up the last few yards to Dduallt with the 1230 Porthmadog-Tanygrisiau four-coach service of 29 May 1979. *Tom Heavyside*

More evidence of suspect drainage – and, probably, recent inclement weather – is seen between the tracks at Dduallt on 23 April 1957, long before the railway was to re-establish itself here. As can be seen, with the station behind the photographer, the original line entered the site through a shallow cutting surmounted by an iron footbridge typical of this stretch of the line, leading up to a farmer's barn as well as being part of a recognised footpath. With the later flooding of the line above Dduallt and the building of the subsequent 'Deviation', this bridge was removed, to be replaced by a completely new version in reinforced concrete, to carry the railway over itself.

Taking a 'longer view', this is the comparative aspect of that bridge, now in full service for the railway. On 5 May 2004 *David Lloyd George* negotiates the climb round 'the spiral' with the 1020 Porthmadog-Blaenau Ffestiniog train, gaining height to clear the reservoir that has drowned the original trackbed on the approach to Tanygrisiau. Note the heightened level of the bridge span, the resultant embankments on either side, and the provision of footpath access underneath the railway, immediately to the right of the supporting pillars beneath *DLG*. Note also the helpful sign, both pointing the way for the footpath and giving indications of approximate walking times for three locations. *Brian Pask/MJS*

These three photographs illustrate the Dduallt station site through the last half-century. In the first, during the 'wilderness years', being so remote from any easy public access, the station slept quietly, largely left to sheep and grass. Around 1950 a visitor rests at the end of the siding, while the original alignment still forges its way directly ahead, through a gate that is now more permanently closed across the rails. In the bright afternoon spring sunshine, the house on the left – curiously not associated with the railway despite its location – is shielded from view by the spreading branches of a neighbouring tree.

To regain the top end of the line at Blaenau Ffestiniog, the railway had to be lifted some 35 feet to circumvent the obstacle of the new reservoir at Tanygrisiau. The solution was the 'Deviation', and the first sod was cut into the hillside on 2 January 1965. Nine months later, on 28 November, a temporary hut has been provided for the volunteers and a skip wagon sits on the track, evidence of work in progress. Otherwise, the nature of the site is little changed, with the house still hidden and the track alignment unaltered.

On 5 May 2004, 40 years of development and progress are self-evident. The original line still forges through the platform like an arrow, but then swings sharply right beyond, immediately before the last telegraph pole in the distance, to negotiate the Deviation. Trees and nature still predominate, but since the felling of the large tree seen above, the house is now visible; a siding remains from the days of the station being a temporary terminus; and the signpost seen opposite stands at the end of the platform. *Brian Hilton, Paul Chancellor collection/Gerald Adams/ MJS*

During its period as a temporary terminus – from 6 April 1968 to 26 May 1975 – Dduallt (whose name means 'black hill') briefly became a hive of activity: as a train arrived, the locomotive ran round, then prepared for departure. On 6 September 1972 the latter two events have occurred and *Merddin Emrys* waits to begin the 1420 return trip to Porthmadog. Note the wooden sales stall, the run-round loop without siding and the house still hidden by the trees.

Six years later the station is no longer the upper terminus of the line. As *Blanche* prepares to depart with a train for Porthmadog, track has been restored a further 2 miles northward, to Tanygrisiau station. Service trains will not return there, however, for a further 26 days, with a temporary terminus on this day – 29 May 1978 – at Llyn Ystradau, alongside the 'enemy', the reservoir holding the old trackbed in its grip. Note how, over the six years from the previous view, the siding has appeared, together with a controlling signal and the provision of a water tank for locos. Common to both views is Observation Coach No 101. *Geoff King/Brian Morrison*

Even though the very early days of restoration saw major effort at the bottom end of the line, the railway still had its eye on the upper reaches, with occasional trains making the long journey through the wilderness to inspect and collect useful materials. One such trip is seen on 23 April 1957. During a brief stop at Dduallt, volunteers and crew of *Moelwyn* – in 'push-pull' mode, with empty slate wagon fore and FR Van No 1 aft – take a break from their toils. Note the house again, uninhabited, on the left.

The second picture is from the busy period for the station, and the original *Earl of Merioneth*, with a head of steam, stands in the platform in August 1969, waiting for the call to begin the journey south from the temporary terminus, while passengers enjoy the sunshine and the nature of the place.

While the house stood empty for many years, it did not suffer major vandalism until the latter years of the 20th century! Sadly, certain elements of our present society cannot leave things alone, leading to the sad sight of it now, virtually 'eyeless' and beyond economic repair. While neither the property nor the direct responsibility of the railway, its dilapidated and deteriorating condition next to the waiting area at the station is not conducive to lifting the spirits of visiting walkers and/or passengers. On 3 May 2004 *Linda* enters the station and prepares to pause as the 1315 Blaenau Ffestiniog-Porthmadog train. *Brian Pask/Dave Southern/MJS*

Outside the house on 27 November 1965, the worksite shows the preparations for the construction of the Deviation, littered with the necessary tools and equipment ready for the volunteers to work their wonders. Note the stone shelf boundary on the right, between railway and house.

The second photograph illustrates a momentous day: the date is 25 May 1982 and the railway is once again open all the way to Blaenau Ffestiniog! *Merddin Emrys* pauses with the 1321 up train, while on the left the coaching stock of the re-opening train, hauled by *Blanche*, stands ready for the 'right away'. The guard of the latter, on the left, looks to see if any passengers intend to 'jump ship' to join his train! Note the small outhouse behind the stone wall of the house on the right, and the wooden 'Bunny Hutch' sales cabin. This had previously served at Tan-y-bwlch, before being moved here, where it still serves the public.

To provide a comparative photograph, *David Lloyd George* pauses briefly at Dduallt with the 1020 up train on 5 May 2004. Note that a stone shelter has been provided and that the trees are ever present and still growing.
Gerald Adams/Peter Treloar/MJS

'Past and present' in one photograph! The original track still follows its original course on the left in this view from 12 October 1975, while to its right the new line curves on to the Deviation. The loop, to the right of the platform, is here joined by a third and fourth track, a temporary shuttle bay, complete with short wooden staging, and a siding. With barrels and cable drums on the platform, work is obviously under way. Note the 'scar' in the tree line in the left distance, where the new, higher alignment has been put in place.

On Sunday 14 November 1976 a new signal box is under construction. *Mary Ann*, complete with 'pagoda' roof, stands alongside while, above, *Blanche* approaches with Brian Hollingsworth's special train. A former BR Civil Engineer, Brian had overseen the Deviation construction and later authored *FR Adventure* – the train seen here was part of the launch of that book. The three onlookers in the right foreground will soon have to move to avoid meeting *Blanche* as she rounds the curve into the station! *Sydney Leleux/Howard Wilson*

Time has moved on and there have been changes at this point, some more obvious than others. Compared to the pictures on page 91, the trees are attempting to regain the space and heal the 'scar'; the rails have been lifted on the original trackbed, but the sleeper marks are still visible on the ground; and walkers are no longer, officially, to use the gateway to access the footpath along and beyond the old alignment. On 3 May 2004 *Linda* sweeps around the Deviation to arrive with the 1315 departure from Blaenau Ffestiniog, seen previously on page 89. Note that the former loop line has been lifted and Dduallt, no longer a passing place, has lost its signal box. *Judi Stretton*

As already stated, the first sod for the spiral was cut in January 1965, and work then continued as fast as the number of volunteers and availability of dynamite would allow! On 27 November 1965 a new cutting is being made at Site 2, on the far side of the hill to the station, with spoil being removed by tipper wagon on temporary trackwork. Wellingtons and hard hats are the order of the day as this group work under a makeshift shelter. A decade of earth-moving and rock-breaking lies ahead of them. *Gerald Adams*

Looking in the opposite direction on the same day, some of the breach in the 'black hill' created by hard graft (and dynamite) in building the Deviation can be seen, showing progress made while work is under way to widen and join Sites 2 and 3, on the opposite side of the hill from the station. Construction had actually begun a few feet behind the camera. *Gerald Adams*

The spiral is finally completed and trains are running up the new alignment. On 28 August 1979 passenger services are now open to Tanygrisiau, 2 miles on from Dduallt, and with the ever-increasing popularity of the railway and resultant growth in passenger numbers, trains are becoming longer! Here *Mountaineer* passes the site of the farmer's stone barn (behind the photographer) with an up train, with the occupants of the leading Third Class open coach no doubt appreciating the warmth of the summer sunshine. Dduallt station, with its signal and oil tank in place, can be seen to the left.

Sixteen years later the view is very largely unchanged, except for the insidious tree growth on and beyond the hill, and the smoothing of the new embankment on which the train is running due to nature's relentless attentions. On 7 June 1995 *Merddin Emrys* – now, thankfully, back in his true shape – climbs away from Dduallt, but this time to travel all the way to Blaenau Ffestiniog. Note that, on the station, a nameboard has appeared, but the signal and water tank have gone. *John Hunt/MJS*

By the Deviation to Tanygrisiau

Having left Dduallt, on the original direct route to Tanygrisiau, the line ran through open countryside to the eastern flank of Moelwyn Bach. Initially this outcrop was surmounted by an inclined plane, but from 1842 the

railway enjoyed a slightly more direct – and certainly easier – approach through Moelwyn Tunnel. This view from 28 August 1973 is looking towards the tunnel, with track still in place, passing under a sheep crossing bridge. Note the dry-stone abutments to the bridge and the similarly constructed walls on either side of the line, protecting it from stray sheep. Moelwyn Mawr can just be seen in the left distance.

By 29 July 1991 the trackbed remains but the rails have been taken up for use elsewhere, leaving behind the sleepers. Members of a course studying the narrow gauge railways of the area at Plas Tan-y-bwlch – together with 'Sebastian' the Papillon! – rest under the bridge on the way back from a visit to the tunnel mouth. Apart from the disappearance of the tracks and some collapse in the wall in the right foreground, relatively little has changed, with the telegraph pole still in situ and only minor amendments to the bridge superstructure. Sadly, into the 21st century, the local farmer has seen fit to block the trackbed, with the bridge decking removed and dumped across the pathway.

Sydney Leleux/MJS

This is the southern entrance to the 730-yard Moelwyn Tunnel of 1842, seen just over a century later, in 1950, with a spot of light at the far end just visible. In the later years of the 19th century a signal stood by the wall on the left to protect movements through the tunnel, operated by a 'tunnel keeper', who presumably enjoyed a pretty lonely existence at this isolated spot!

As has already been noted, several trips were made to the upper reaches of the line in the early days, before the reservoir was built. While these were sometimes jolly good fun, they always had a serious purpose – collecting wagons, rails, telegraph poles, points and anything else that might be of use. *Moelwyn* is seen on one such expedition, about to enter the tunnel on its way to Blaenau. Manager Allan Garraway at the helm is accompanied by Paul Dukes, later Manager at Boston Lodge. *Brian Hilton, Paul Chancellor collection/John Alexander, MJS collection*

In many ways the northern portal of the tunnel looked very similar to the southern end, with only the cutting being slightly deeper. This view from 27 October 1954 shows the potential problems with drainage, with recent rainfall still lying between the rails. Eight years after closure, the trackbed otherwise looks in good condition, despite colonisation by coarse grasses.

Rails through the tunnel were lifted over the New Year of 1962, in connection with work on the new reservoir, the lower part of which would reach this point. In this view from 12 April 1975 the reservoir is in existence but is obviously at 'low tide', allowing access to the photographer. Note the water still present, however, in the bottom left and the virtual disappearance of the tunnel mouth, with just the top coping stones visible. *Central Electric Authority/Sydney Leleux*

97

Opposite The flooding of the original course of the railway left the restorationists with a dilemma. Much 'midnight oil' was burned in considering the options for forward progress, the final decision being to steer to the west of the waters on a completely new alignment. Looking north on 14 April 1973, all three routes – old and new – are visible. The Deviationists' mess hut on the right graces the 1842 trackbed immediately south of the tunnel mouth, while in the centre the course of the 1836 horse-drawn incline can be seen as a rutted pathway being descended by two walkers. To the left, early 'scrapings' are just visible where the new railway will eventually run.

Exactly two years later, the 1836 incline is still clearly visible but now dominated by the emerging new alignment. On 12 April 1975 the new tunnel is being carved from the hillside (top left), with temporary track laid to assist access and removal of spoil. Tipper wagons wait for their next duty. *Both Sydney Leleux*

Another 18 months have passed and progress is obvious in this view, looking south. At the location known as 'Two Trees', a base camp – colloquially known as 'the football pitch'! – has been established, together with an access road from the 1836 trackbed on the left. With the 1842 line still present, centre left, to give inspiration, the operation was both professional and impressive. The right-hand siding, on a slightly elevated alignment, accepted the full skips – hauled by small diesel *Diana* – from where the stone from the cutting was tipped to a grid of rails, where it was then broken to smaller dimensions and passed through a crusher and grader and on to a conveyor. This was no amateurish affair, however, with professional miners being supported by railway staff as work proceeded six days a week, volunteers assisting when available. *Howard Wilson*

Above left Turning to look north again, the view up the line in 1976 clearly shows the magnitude of the task, with prodigious volumes of rock already extracted from the hillside to form the cutting towards the southern entrance of the new tunnel. The temporary track, complete with passing loop, leads into the tunnel, with scaffolding around the mouth and cables taking air and electricity into the darkness to facilitate ongoing work. While the initial plan to flood the old route was met with disappointment and anger, it has proved to be a blessing in disguise, for this new tunnel has since served the railway far better than the restricted gauge and damp conditions of the old one would have done. An appropriate warning sign (bottom left) guards access to the tunnel. *Gerald Adams*

Left Inside looking out, on 14 November 1976, the battered Jubilee track meanders out towards the 'football pitch', with the entrance scaffolding highlighted against the sky. *Howard Wilson*

Above This view of the tunnel base camp area was taken from the hillside above the workings, again demonstrating the sheer depth of the new trackbed within the rising ground. On 12 April 1975 the excavation work is still in its early days, with only the approach cutting dug and the track not settled into its later course, although a more permanent rail alignment has obviously been laid up to 'Two Trees' as, in the distance, *Blanche* has brought a trainload of visitors, who are making their way to the site. *Sydney Leleux*

Right A similar view, but a celebratory occasion: the date is 25 June 1977, the tunnel opening day, and assembled guests watch with joy and anticipation as the time approaches to cut the ribbon. In the background *Merddin Emrys* gently simmers, proudly adorned with a defiant 'Blaenau Ffestiniog Here We Come!' headboard. It is interesting to see some of the fashions on display and, another sign of the times, the impressive number of youthful beards being sported amongst the crowd! *Peter Treloar*

Up and over the 1836 inclined planes, the view of the reservoir comes into view on the right, with the original trackbed still just visible in the centre as a meandering pathway. To the left of this 12 April 1975 photograph, north of the new tunnel works, the way ahead is being crafted on the new, raised alignment; a stone embankment has been created part way and a rudimentary cutting made into the hillside flank just beyond. The power station buildings can be seen in the sunshine beyond the reservoir.

Sunshine again graces the view on 3 May 2004, showing how nature has healed the scars cut by the railway, leading to the impression that the landscape has always been this way! Two walkers pause to review the scene and possibly to wait for and watch the passage of a train, while the Claytons' two Papillons, although well used to local train travel, are presumably more interested in their walk! *Sydney Leleux/MJS*

All three of the railway's routes are again seen here. On 28 August 1994 *Merddin Emrys* heads the nine-coach 1045 Porthmadog departure past Llyn Ystradau, about to pass above the power station buildings, just out of the picture to the left. To the left of the train, the 1842 tunnel alignment veers away from the new route, while the 1836 horse-drawn way climbs over the hill and the present route zigzags around the contours above them both. The viewpoint of the photographs opposite is on the upper bend of the 1836 route, seen in the middle distance. In the 1970s a temporary halt was located just to the right of the train while the Tanygrisiau station site was being fashioned. *Peter Treloar*

Looking towards Tanygrisiau, this vantage point is roughly opposite the end of the straight, behind *Merddin*'s train above. On 3 May 2004 *Earl of Merioneth* has the easier task, running downhill with the 1150 Blaenau Ffestiniog-Porthmadog service. The 11 coaches demonstrate the need to cope with the ever-increasing traffic numbers into the 21st century. With the reservoir level much higher here, the original trackbed can still just be seen as a footpath around the edge of the waters. The slab of the main power station buildings dominates the left-hand background, with Tanygrisiau just visible beyond. *MJS*

Opposite One of the trademarks of this photographer's work is the foresight and determination to escape from the traditional view and to capture one with greater dramatic potential, placing the train well within its landscape. Despite the dull lighting conditions of the late afternoon of 29 August 1986, the diminutive size of the train – and its lazy smoke trail – the sinuous nature of both rail and road and the magnificence of the background outcrops all lead to a very satisfying vista. *Linda* has left the summit of the line and coasts tender-first downhill as the 1745 service from Blaenau Ffestiniog, about to pass the power station, just visible bottom right. The roadway from the latter is the original 1836 railway route, now subsumed beneath tarmac. *Peter Treloar*

What is now that roadway is seen here in its former glory, complete with the siding to Wrysgan Quarry incline to the left. Around 1950 two walkers, complete with rucksacks on their backs, survey the scene, including the abandoned empty slate wagon on the left and the equally abandoned stone building below them to the right. The stone embankment of an earlier FR alignment accompanies the curve of the railway towards Tanygrisiau station. Note the white plume of the waterfall in the distance.

The apparent incorrectness of this equivalent view of 5 May 2004 is due to the blasting of rock and the realignment of the road to the power station – behind the camera – after the railway had been lifted. The waterfall still follows its age-old path, here behind the café next to the visitor centre, while the new roadway utilises the course of the old siding. The curving trackbed and wall have been dispensed with, the waters now lapping up to the resultant shallow embankment and the new railway passing behind and above the power station visitor centre. *Brian Hilton, Paul Chancellor collection/MJS*

As well as needing the new Moelwyn Tunnel on the new run up the line, the FR also had to carve a passage through the hillside behind and above the power station. It is still early days after this achievement on 29 May 1979 as *Blanche* negotiates the last few hundred yards of the new route and the bare earth and scar on the rock face are still painfully apparent. Heads poke from engine and carriages as the eight-coach load, bound for Tanygrisiau, is about to pass the perfunctory trespassing notice.

Sixteen years later, some of those scars are healing. Grass is reclaiming and softening the cutting sides and even the rock face seems to have weathered, although still highly visible. On 9 June 1995, with driver Colin Dukes at the controls, *Merddin Emrys* again demonstrates the growth in traffic over the years, by now having ten coaches behind him on his way to the terminus at Blaenau Festiniog. *Tom Heavyside/MJS*

Following the course of the line towards Tanygrisiau, it crosses the road leading up the hillside, controlled by lights and warning siren, although the open nature of the location gives plenty of notice to road users of the approach of the train. In the mid-1980s *Linda* threads her way along the narrow-gauge trackbed, over the crossing and on to the station, with a rake of cherry-red-liveried coaches.

In distinctly less pleasant weather – in fact, driving rain! – *Linda* is again seen at the crossing, this time with a rake of maroon and cream coaching stock, hauling the 1020 service from Porthmadog on the final approach to Tanygrisiau station. The red warning lights shine brightly in the gloom on 6 May 2004, as the low cloud threatens to blanket all in view, leaving the car in no doubt as to the necessary course of action. *Peter Treloar/MJS*

Tanygrisiau

Looking at the Tanygrisiau station site today, it is heard to imagine how different both the layout and the ambience once were. Admittedly seen in its latter days, after the railway had closed and the site had been abandoned, left to the vagaries of the weather and the unhelpful designs of the local populace, this view, looking west on 21 August 1961, gives a very fair indication of the state of affairs. The station waiting shelter now houses alternative visitors, with one of their number burnt out on the right, while immediately to the left of the shelter the old goods shed looks uncared for and unkempt, with an even shabbier neighbour nearer the camera. Tracks are still visible on the right, close to the drunken telegraph pole.

On an equally dull 4 May 2004, the view and atmosphere is wholly altered, due to the necessity of carving out a halt at a higher level than of yore. The old goods shed remains – now repaired and weather-proofed – but now with the new, elevated trackbed up to its waist; a new signal box has been constructed almost on the site of the old station building; an island platform has been installed; and the up track (right) takes a course excavated from the earlier rockface. Trees now provide a screen for the dam and power station. *Sydney Leleux/MJS*

These three views of the station illustrate the redevelopment over the past three decades. Though much work has obviously been undertaken in the first photograph, it is still in the early days of reconstruction at the site. With both Jubilee track and motorised crane in place to move concrete for a new culvert – in active use in this photograph – this westward view on 29 March 1975 shows that much of the land beyond the immediate worksite is still undisturbed. Concentration here is on the provision of the station site and the building of a culvert beneath the trackbed.

One year later the land beyond has now well and truly been disturbed! With a variety of machines in the middle distance, a quartet of visitors survey the scene beyond, appraising the area where pre-stressed concrete beams will form a bridge to carry the railway across the Afon Cwmorthin. Note the two houses, right and left, common to both views, and more temporary Jubilee track helping with removal of spoil.

The date of the third picture is 4 May 2004 and the site is largely complete, with only minor adjustments now necessary to satisfy any operational concerns. The white house still overlooks the scene on the right, while that on the left has been extended. Track is once again gracing the down platform on the left, and posts are in position for the erection of section signalling, ready for the loop to be put into use to increase operational flexibility one month after this view. *Sydney Leleux/ Howard Wilson/MJS*

Illustrating the changing fortunes of the line towards Blaenau Ffestiniog, the first photograph shows the railway long abandoned on 27 October 1954; there is seemingly no hope of a return of trains and the track is fighting a rearguard action against the encroaching grass. While some of the locals had utilised the line for their own purposes, the neighbouring houses were undisturbed by trains.

By 1961, while still visible, the right-hand turnout from the main line had been cut short and the siding on the right completely removed, together with the rails and the wagon for re-use elsewhere. Five years later evidence of a railway is all but obliterated in this view from August 1966. Washing hangs on a makeshift line by the boundary wall while – strangely, considering there are no trains – safety fencing has been placed on the top of the footbridge!

On 4 May 2004 all around is much as before, but on the ground the raised level of the railway can be judged by the boundary wall on the right, now virtually flush with the surrounding railway land. The bridge has also been raised and given new decking, and other signs of progress are the rendering and provision of dormer windows on the houses on the right. Out of view, just below the house on the hill, Dolrhedyn Bridge crosses a steep, narrow and twisting road. It was removed in 1957 by the local council, who agreed to reinstate it should it become necessary. To their cost, this happened in 1980, when a new bridge – raised and much strengthened – was put in place, in conjunction with the progress towards Blaenau. This was at no cost to the railway, but the rock fall slightly further up the line at Penlan did present the restorationists with challenges both physical and financial! *Central Electricity Board/Howard Wilson/MJS*

The view back from that footbridge in August 1966 looks across to the power station and reservoir, now completed and operational. On the railway, locals park their cars, accessed by a steep incline from the road below; the station building is semi-dismantled; the loop turnout has been cut; and on the right residents of the houses have given themselves direct access to the trackbed.

The date is now 1980 and the final push is on to restore the running line into Blaenau Ffestiniog. The level has been raised, track and concrete trunking laid, a basic island platform installed and rock cleared to give access to up trains. The houses on the right have had their frontages improved and fencing re-instated.

By 4 May 2004 the railway has been running along its full length for a little over 20 years and the locals have settled into the routine of having trains passing their front doors once more. Detail differences are visible, such as rendering and rails guarding the parking space, but the major development – apart from the reduction of the rockface on the right and the appearance of a signal box – is the growth of the conifers hiding the view of the power station. *Howard Wilson (2)/MJS*

As the railway passes through the village of Tanygrisiau it snakes along a rock shelf above and between rows of houses. In the days before the railway regained access to this part of the route, in the late summer of 1970, the undisturbed nature of the structure is clear, with grass and missing coping stones the main evidence. Some of Blaenau's massive deposits of slate waste are visible in the distance, the result of more than a century of excavation.

By the time of the second view, 25 years later on 7 June 1995, much progress has been made both on and off the railway. In addition to the very professional-looking trackbed, weed free and with new boundary slabs, the surrounding houses have reacted to changing fashions and refurbishments. Note how tree growth here has enhanced the aesthetics, and the main slate waste heap seems to have softened, while removal of the Glanydon tip has revealed another, on the right.

Jon Marsh/MJS

112

Departing from the buildings, the rock shelf continues onwards, describing an arc to the right to avoid the rocky outcrop. Seen in the first picture around 1950, the diminutive shed seen at the end of the terrace opposite is again in view, looking in receipt of some recent attention.

Some years later and slightly further back, we are now looking up Barlwyd Terrace and can see the result of nature's trackbed reclamation, together with some disturbance of the coping stones. The shed also looks a little less pristine!

As access to the trackbed is now both unavailable and dangerous, this is a comparative view on 4 May 2004, using a long zoom lens from the bridge vantage point used opposite. The old shed still lives on, now with corrugated iron side cladding; the trackbed is clean, with new boundary slabs; and protective fencing is provided on either side of the shallow embankment around the curve. *Brian Hilton, Paul Chancellor collection/MJS collection/MJS*

On the final approaches to Blaenau Ffestiniog, at the 13-mile point from Porthmadog, the railway passes the original 1836 alignment that ran to the old FR's terminus at Dinas. That route marches straight ahead, through the centre of this undated view, towards the massive slate waste deposit that has swamped the trackbed between here and the original terminus. The gateway on the left once gave access to a siding to the incline for Nidd y Gigfran quarry, while the later route swings right, over the Afon Barlwyd.

In the late summer of 1970 only the subsequent growth of grass gives an indication of the passage of time; otherwise, nothing has changed.

By 6 June 1995 the place is very different. The railway has regained its path; the Afon Barlwyd bridge has been re-decked, reduced in width and fenced; landscaping has obliterated the old 1836 alignment; and the boundary walls on both sides have been rebuilt. A level crossing warning signboard has also been erected. *MJS collection/ Jon Marsh/MJS*

The final – and very attractive – view in this section is from a very little-used vantage point, across the road from the railway and up the slope behind the houses. On 6 September 1984 *Earl of Merioneth* heads across the Barlwyd bridge with the 1125 train from Porthmadog, fast approaching its destination in Blaenau Ffestiniog. An old Nidd y Gigfran incline cascades down the side of the hill, stopping abruptly at the area of landscaping, to the left of which is Groesffordd, a house that once enjoyed a model railway in its grounds, but which was burned down in the late 1990s. *Tom Heavyside*

Blaenau Ffestiniog

On the final approach to Blaenau Ffestiniog, the railway passes through the small hamlet of Glan-y-Pwll. The original FR built an engine shed here, sandwiched between the main running line and the 1899 spur to Dinas station, to service this northern end of the line. Until the 1930s it housed the 'Top Shunter', responsible for marshalling trains of slate for the descent to Porthmadog or Minffordd, and provided the loco for the first down passenger train of the day. During the 1940s it was let as a sawmill, but by the summer of 1970 it was certainly in need of some TLC! When considering the resumption of services to this end of the line, the structure gave the restorationists both opportunity and challenge.

By 11 October 1974 the yard has been cleared, tracks re-laid – including on the course of the 1899 route, curving to the left – and the shed is back in use, with one portal closed with stone and a rudimentary door to the other, although still without a roof. At this time, as a gesture of intent to return to Blaenau, the track between here and Tanygrisiau had been re-laid, though yet to be ballasted and finished. Four volunteers pose on *Diana* during a period of skip wagon shunting.

By 4 May 2004 the vista is vastly altered. Still very much in use by the present FR – and even gaining in value to the railway as it develops – the shed has become a much grander affair, complete with an extension on the left and a grand roof to cover it all. Its door has been replaced by a roller shutter – complete with an explicit warning symbol! – and the yard is now in such constant usage that space has become ever more at a premium. *Jon Marsh/Sydney Leleux/ MJS*

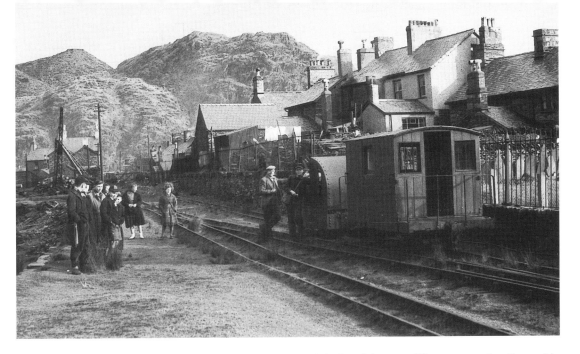

In this rare view from restoration days, the site of Glan-y-Pwll shed and the sawmill's cranes can be glimpsed in the left distance, while *Mary Ann*, complete with van, makes a first run over the line from Boston Lodge to this northern outpost in March 1955. Some nine years after the railway was abandoned, the sight of a train at this location has obviously caused a great deal of commotion, judging by the number of local schoolchildren standing by the trackside, viewing what the visitors have done and are about to do! No doubt the householders on the right never expected to have their tranquillity disturbed in this, admittedly genteel, way!

On 6 May 2004 the view is instantly recognisable. The housing is still the same, with only detail differences, most notably the addition of a dormer window and the removal of one or two chimneys. In the pouring rain, *Linda*'s crew keep an eye on the photographer from the comfort of their cab as they begin the long run back to Porthmadog with the 1150 departure from Blaenau. *Bob Smallman/MJS*

The twin-gabled house seen to the left of the views on the previous page, once occupied by railway staff and now utilised as a volunteer hostel, stands by the level crossing on the road from Tanygrisiau. This view in August 1970, over the crossing gate, does not look promising from a railway point of view. Completely abandoned since the few expeditions to recover rails and wagons in the mid-1950s, grasses are doing a grand job in disguising the permanent way, and on the left a rhododendron stakes a claim. On either side the stone walls still look in fine condition. The footbridge served the former Glan-y-Pwll School.

By 6 June 1995, despite only one track now in use, the whole ambience of the site has changed for the better. A gateway, fencing and wooden cattle grid have been erected to prevent access on to the now restored railway, the right-hand wall has had a coping added, the telegraph pole has been re-sited, and the bridge span has been raised and replaced. Observation coach No 101 brings up the rear of a train on the last yards of its run to Blaenau, full of, hopefully, appreciative passengers. Today the view is little changed, except for the removal of the tree to the right of the bridge, and the latter being closed to the public. *Jon Marsh/MJS*

Around the corner from the views opposite, the original railway headed for Blaenau Ffestiniog and its final terminus at Duffws. Its straight course at this point was paralleled by the track into the former LNWR/LMS terminus, the cream bricks of whose entrance can just be seen on the extreme left. Between 1881 and 1939 the FR had a station here, situated by the slab of walling seen to the left of the track in the middle distance. In this view from 4 April 1959, a road has been built across the trackbed, precluding any immediate return to the centre of town along the old route under the distant footbridge, but the old water tower and signal post stand as encouragement.

This is the same vista but a whole different view! The cream brickwork can still be seen on the left, despite the station being closed since 1982, and the stone wall still protects road from rail, but otherwise the layout is dramatically altered. The coming of the revitalised railway has caused the raising and redesigning of the 'new'

roadway into town, with even an extra portal in the event of the railway wishing to install a second line. Gorse bushes now mark the site of the old FR station and a flower bed fashioned out of old sleepers aims to enliven the view, with a 'host of golden daffodils' enjoying yet more pouring rain on 4 May 2004. *Gerald Adams/MJS*

Top Looking in the opposite direction, the water tower seen on the previous page is in the distance in this view closer to the town, showing the aforementioned FR station, known as Stesion Fain. Seen in the 1950s, when the enthusiasts were descending on the moribund railway, the station canopy is gradually deteriorating, and the track gradually being covered by grass. Happily, when the site was abandoned as the new railway concentrated on restoring the lower end of the route, the canopy was not destroyed, but was purchased to begin a new life as a football stand in nearby Manod. Note the footbridge by Glan-y-Pwll just visible on the extreme left, the cream brickwork echoing that at the ex-LNWR/LMS station across the road, and the rarely photographed iron gate on the right. *Bob Smallman*

Middle Looking across the site, the old station canopy stood roughly in line with the second, third and fourth coaches of this up train. It is the opening day to Blaenau and the interim worksite is still in position in the foreground. *Linda* helps to make history, returning FR trains to the centre of Blaenau Ffestiniog. *Peter Treloar*

Bottom Seen from the other side of the track, *Merddin Emrys* is heading away from the town under the new bridge, one of those purpose-built for the railway's extension into Blaenau. The extent of groundworks involved can be judged by the open landscaping yet to be softened by time and nature. The road now gives a wider and more direct access to Tanygrisiau and beyond. *Norman Kneale*

These three photographs show the extensive slate exchange sidings, adjacent to the standard gauge station. The first was taken less than a month before the outbreak of the Second World War, when life was turned upside down, but the sidings are continuing their long-standing trade, with stacks of slate piled awaiting despatch. Note the houses alongside Llwyn-y-Gell Road and the slate waste heaps beyond, in this view from 14 August 1939.

By the date of the second picture, July 1960, the basic layout is little changed, with only relatively minor detail differences. Housing is much as before, the bulky point levers remain, and slate still occupies its traditional place, again awaiting onward transport – though by road, rather than the FR, by this time. Note the glimpse of the standard gauge cattle and horse dock, bottom left.

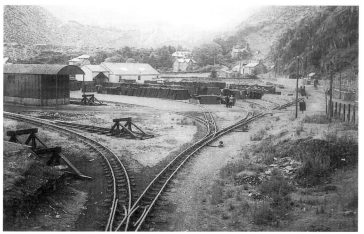

A comparative view was given in Volume 1 (page 67), so here we have a view from near the same vantage point, but looking to the left towards the standard gauge station, whose buildings and platform are visible in the centre distance, 20 years after they were abandoned, following the opening of the new facilities in the centre of town. As can be seen, the station site has largely been abandoned and the sidings area given over to industrial use. *Robin Butterell/Percy Pike collection/MJS*

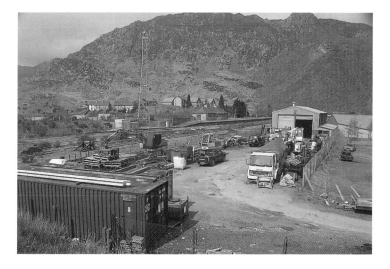

In its heyday, Blaenau was served by two standard gauge railways, the LNWR/LMS – already seen – and the GWR. The route of the FR ran between the two termini – south of the LNWR and north of the GWR – thus preventing any junction between the two. This early 1950s view shows the approach to the GWR station. In the foreground is the GWR headshunt, crossed by FR rails leading into the goods and slate exchange yard, hidden by the wall. The GWR goods shed, with doors of different sizes to suit the wagons, is in the centre distance, with the passenger station to its left. The FR served the left-hand face of the platform, passing under the footbridge then Queens Bridge on its way to its terminus at Duffws. The white-painted Queen's Hotel is beyond the GWR station.

With the seemingly unstoppable northern progress by the restorationists in the late 1970s, plans were agreed to re-site the LNWR/LMS 'Conwy Valley' station to an area by the Queen's Hotel and to have the new FR station alongside where the old GWR passenger lines had once been, thereby providing an easy interchange between the two. This gave the new FR a straight run into the complex, as can be seen from this view. Six years after the railway returned to the town, *Prince* restarts the run downhill in July 1988, from the still developing station, while a connecting DMU stands in the standard gauge platform on the left. Note that all of the former GWR buildings and sidings have been lost, with a school now occupying the latter. *MJS collection/Terry Gough*

A closer view of the GWR station – Blaenau Ffestiniog (Central) – on 14 August 1958 shows the 2.20pm train for Bala waiting to leave in the right-hand standard gauge platform, with the redundant FR tracks to the left, passing through the stone-faced cutting to pass under Queen's Bridge to terminate a few yards further on at Duffws. The Queen's Hotel, on slightly higher ground, dominates the scene, with the GWR terminus dwarfed by comparison.

The new 1982 stations dramatically remodelled the site. Though not an exact recreation of the above shot, the stone wall on the left roughly approximates to that seen above, with the platform occupying the old trackbed and the Conwy Valley DMU on what was part of the previous expanse of platform. The Queen's Hotel still overlooks affairs, visible through the footbridge that joins the railway to the main street through the town. On 17 September 2003 First North Western-liveried single car No 153363 is viewed from the FR platform, waiting to return up the branch to Llandudno Junction. *P. Waylett, Peter Johnson collection/MJS*

The new arrangement has been open for three months and Bristol Railway Circle is paying a visit on 30 August 1982. The excursion train fully occupies the standard gauge platform, as Class 47 No 47539 – named *Rochdale Pioneers* three months later – runs round ready for the return trip. In the FR station *Mountaineer* waits to haul a delayed 1435 departure to Porthmadog. Note the school building on the left, built on the former GWR sidings.

With the Moelwyns to the west of the town still providing a dramatic backdrop, *Earl of Merioneth* stands in the FR platform, having just arrived with the 1020 train from Porthmadog. On either side of the railway little has changed apart from some tree growth, although two decades of progress show a huge difference on the FR in this view from 4 May 2004. As well as protective fencing now in place on the school wall, there is now a substantial waiting canopy, complete with sales kiosk; a water tower has appeared at the Porthmadog end of the station, together with newly erected colour light signals; and a line has been installed on the town side of the platform. *Peter Treloar/MJS*

This view of the relatively new FR station in July 1988 was taken from the Conwy Valley line platform. A six-car DMU rests in the latter – an unusual length for the Valley trains – while *Mountaineer* has run round its train and prepares to make the long run back to Porthmadog, with Observation Car No 100 immediately behind it. The Queen's Hotel still dominates the left-of-centre view, with its clean white paintwork.

Once again the dramatic changes are on the FR's station, with the affixing of a station nameboard being the only real change on the standard gauge side. On 4 May 2004 *Earl of Merioneth* runs round its coaches before taking water and returning to Porthmadog. Note the few observers, the day after a Bank Holiday in poor weather conditions. *Terry Gough/MJS*

Our final destination is the centre of Blaenau Ffestiniog and the building that once served the station known as Duffws. The station name means 'precipice' in English – highly appropriate when one considers the mass of rock and slate behind! Note the incline to Votty Quarry on the left. As can be seen in this view on 3 August 1973, the once proud station building is still serving the public but now ignominiously providing a different type of convenience! With the old platform side facing the car park, the siding space beyond has become a council depot.

Happily, the building and the neighbouring houses still stand. Attempts have been made to tidy the area; the light industrial usage has been cleared away; the car park has seen enlargement and some redesigning; and trees have been planted. Sadly, this improvement is somewhat counteracted by the unsightly recycling bins, in a scene not enlivened by yet more torrential rain on 4 May 2004. *Sydney Leleux/MJS*

And so we say farewell to this second 'Past and Present' volume of Ffestiniog Railway views. The guard gives a wave to acknowledge the train's – and our – departure, appropriately showing us that we are looking at the last vehicle! On 30 September 1995 *Prince* leaves Tan-y-bwlch with the 1355 down freight, consisting mostly of empty slate wagons. *Peter Treloar*

INDEX